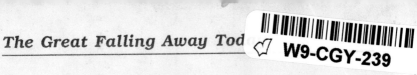

The
Great
Falling
Away
Today

By Milton Green

Be Fruitful and Multiply Ministries
P.O. Box 3459 • Palestine, Texas 75802

Be Fruitful and Multiply Ministries
P.O. Box 3459, Palestine, Texas 75802

Library of Congress Catalog Card Number 86-81359

ISBN Number 0-910311-40-4

All scripture references are from the New American Standard Version
unless otherwise indicated.

Typography by Publications Technologies
Printed in the United States of America

Table of Contents

Introduction ----------------------------- 7

1. The Alarming Condition
   of the Church Today —
   Apostasy ----------------------------- 11

2. The Nature of Satan
   or the Nature of God -------------------- 20

3. The Law and the Powers
   of Darkness Today -------------------- 36

4. The Falling Away and
   the Fiery Trials ------------------------- 84

5. The Harlot Church Today ---------------- 108

6. The Prophets of Old
   Spoke of These Days ----------------- 130

7. False Teachers Today -------------------- 136

8. Hear the Word of the Lord,
   You Rulers of Sodom ----------------- 161

9. Wake Up, Wake Up,
   Sleeping Virgins --------------------- 167

10. Rebuilding the Temple
    in These Last Days ------------------- 198

Afterword ----------------------------- 213

"If I must have some failing, let me rather speak the truth with too great severity than once to act the hypocrite and conceal the truth."

— Anonymous

Introduction

Many Christians believe we are living in a time of one of the greatest revivals in the history of the church. Evangelism reports from around the world seem to substantiate this claim. Manifestations of supernatural gifts, signs, and wonders are commonplace in a large percentage of churches. They are widely proclaimed as being from the Lord and proof that God is well pleased with the church today.

Ministries are expanding into mass media evangelism which spans the globe. Evangelistic and charismatic groups are experiencing tremendous numerical growth as new buildings can be seen springing up and spreading out in almost every direction.

All of these things would seem to refute the remote possibility that we are now living in the time of the *great falling away of the church:* a falling away from true faith and the lifestyle which God demands of His people and which is taught in scripture. Instead, multitudes of church members say they are eagerly anticipating the return of Christ through a secret rapture which will whisk them out of every trial and the tribulation which is obviously coming upon the world.

However, when close investigation is made of the personal lives of the church members, we find little difference between most of their lifestyles and those of people in the world. Divorce, adultery, homosexuality, gossip, unforgiveness, strife, jealousy, outbursts of anger, disputes, and factions are as prevalent in the churches today as they are in the world.

Almost any pastor or church leader you talk to privately will admit that down inside he knows something is desperately wrong. Many people wander from church to church looking for something they know they are missing. The message of "peace and safety" being preached cannot put an end to their inner turmoil. They discern the spiritual emptiness in religious traditions and often fall prey to cults and sects that draw them away from Jesus Christ and the Word of God altogether. Others are looking for the true body of Christ which they know is supposed to be "holy and blameless." People easily become disillusioned when they see in the church what they see in the world.

Churches have turned to recreation and entertainment in an attempt to hold the people, becoming more and more like the world. Rather than select a pastor on the basis of his spiritual maturity and understanding, they choose a man based on his fundraising ability and his charismatic personality to attract people in order to increase the size of the congregation and "build the church."

Counseling ministries flourish as the message proclaimed by the churches is not sufficient to meet the needs of the spiritually hungry and desperate people. Many pastors, looking for answers, have investigated other denominations and groups (sometimes secretly for fear of being labeled disloyal to their denomination), only to be disappointed to find the other groups have similar spiritual problems.

In the midst of this day of people searching for answers, we should recognize that we are now experiencing what the Lord promised would come. " 'Behold, days are coming,' declares the Lord God, 'when I will *send a famine* on the land, *not a famine for bread* or a thirst for water, but rather for *hearing the words of the Lord*. And people will *stagger* (in spiritual darkness) from sea to sea, and from the north even to the east; they will go to and fro to seek the word of the Lord, but *they will not find it* " Amos 8:11, 12.

While this famine continues, the Lord has begun to awaken His sheep and reveal to them the essential truths from His Word that have been overlooked and ignored. God did not find it necessary to cooperate with the requirements of religious systems in order to reveal His truths in the time of Jesus. That has not changed.

If you are one of those who realize that something has been wrong in your own life and in the lives of those with whom you fellowship, you will find in this book some of the answers you are looking for, answers directly from the Word of God.

As you come to God seeking light and truth, you will realize that we are truly waking from a nightmare of destruction. It is our desire that you will hear His voice through His Word and that you will be faithful to follow Him as He leads His true church out of spiritual darkness.

My motive in writing this book is simply to build up the body of Christ in love. God is using my part to lay a foundation in the life of the believer, a foundation they must have before they can walk with the Lord Jesus Christ in freedom and victory.

God has begun restoring the power and truth of the gospel today. This is the day that will see the glory and power of God coming to earth into His church which will be holy and blameless.

The Alarming Condition of the Church Today — Apostasy

We are now living in the time of the apostasy, the great falling away: "... For it (the day of the Lord) will not come unless the apostasy (falling away from the faith) comes first ..." (II Thess. 2:3).

"Falling away" simply means that a people turn away from faith in God and begin trusting other things. These other things become idols in their hearts, "golden calves," which they depend on to lead them through this life and then into heaven.

People in apostasy begin calling something church which is not *the church*. They begin calling people Christians who are not Christians. In almost every funeral service today, sermons are preached as though the person had gone to heaven. But the Bible says, "The gate is small and the way is narrow that leads to life, and few are those who find it" (Matt. 7:14).

When the children of Israel saw that Moses, their visible leader, delayed to come down from the holy mountain, they tore off their gold rings and brought them to Aaron. Then Aaron took the gold and "fashioned it with a graving tool and made it into a molten calf (to please men); and they said, 'This is your God, O Israel' " (Ex. 32:1-4).

The fleshly hearts of the children of Israel needed a god they could see with their eyes and one which did not impose discipline upon them. Then they could fulfill their fleshly desires and be religious, too. So it is today.

Traditions Replace
the Word of God

Many of the organizational and doctrinal structures of today began as genuine works of the Spirit of God. The Spirit moved Martin Luther through the Word of God and he received a fresh word from the Lord for his day. As the "new light" (new for his day) was spreading, more and more people saw the truths Martin Luther had seen. These people gathered around this light and treated it as if it were the whole gospel. The result was the formation of a religious structure, doctrinally and organizationally, which later became the Lutheran denomination. Generally speaking, those who follow Luther will only accept the light he had. The amazing truth is that if Martin Luther were alive today, he would be diligently seeking more light from the Word of God. Almost every religious structure in existence today began in this same way.

Many of the traditions developed by religious structures were started with good motives. Through the years they have become ritualized and today the Holy Spirit can rarely work through them any longer.

For example, the "mourner's bench" was used by the Holy Spirit during the ministry of Charles Finney.* People would come in repentance and prayer to seek God for hours or days, until their hearts were changed by the Spirit and power of God. Then the Salvation Army used the mourner's bench to call thousands to repentance. Today the mourner's bench has been replaced with "walking the aisle" and

---

*Charles G. Finney, An Autobiography, Revell Publishers, Inc.

"praying the prayer." It is seldom with brokenness or true repentance of the heart that people come to God today.

The hearts of unregenerate church members by the millions blindly trust their doctrines and traditions which have become their idols to lead them to heaven. By so doing they have blinded themselves to many of the truths of God's Word. People whose hearts are set on the flesh nature need a physical, tangible god. Today this need is fulfilled through "a form of godliness" manifested by many religious organizations and doctrinal structures. These, like the golden calf, have been fashioned by the hands of religious leaders of the past to please men and they are protected by the religious leaders of today.

The hearts of the people are captured by partial truths and slogans.

Years of teaching only scriptures that fit into a doctrinal structure have blinded them to the other parts of the gospel and have given them a false security. They can only see in the Bible the part of the Bible which fits into their particular structure.

Like the Pharisees, they are offended when they hear the other parts of the Bible.

When the Word of God is resisted, Jesus becomes a rock of offense and a stumbling stone!

"... 'The stone which the builders rejected, this has become the very cornerstone' and 'a stone of stumbling and a rock of offense,' for they stumble because they are disobedient to the word ..." (I Pet. 2:7, 8).

Tunnel Vision and Doctrines of Men

When we look at the Word of God from any standpoint other than God's point of view, it is tunnel vision.

Tunnel vision causes us to gather around only a part of the Word of God rather than the whole counsel of God. In addition, we will develop attitudes like the Pharisees, "We have all the light."

Their religious structure then becomes an idol in their hearts. They cannot be led out of darkness because they will not receive any new light.

This is exactly how an idol in someone's heart causes a veil to be over their face today. They do not have spiritual eyes to see, or ears to hear and they cannot understand God's Word.

God tells us in Ezekiel 14:3: "Son of man, these men (the elders of Israel — the religious leaders) have set up their idols in their hearts, and have put right before their eyes the stumbling block of their iniquity (a veil). Should I be consulted by them at all?"

Since the Pharisees loved their structure more than Jesus, the words Jesus spoke could have no place in their hearts; their religious structure had their hearts.

If God had had their hearts, they would have received the whole counsel of God's Word and would have been led out of darkness.

However, they could not receive any new light because they thought they already had all the light.

Therefore they did not have ears to hear, eyes to see, nor could they understand the rest of the Bible because their structure had become their whole source of truth.

Many cannot be led out of spiritual darkness today because their hearts have become too hardened by resisting the Word.

Jesus said to the Pharisees: "Why do you not understand what I am saying? It is because you cannot hear My word" (John 8:43).

They could not hear because they had taken only part of the Word of God and built a religious structure which captured their hearts.

They could not receive any new light because the words Jesus spoke would not fit into their religious structure which had their hearts.

Towers of Babel
(Confusion) Today

In Genesis 11:1-7 the goal of the people who built the Tower of Babel was to build their own city and a tower into heaven. They said: "We will use bricks and tar and *make a name for ourselves.*" Their motivation was pride and the result was confusion (that is what Babel means). This is where they all began to speak a different language.

How different is it today? Everyone is going to the same place but they are all speaking a different language. Go downtown in almost any city and see the high corner towers (Zeph. 1:15, 16). In one corner tower the people will tell you, "I was baptized at birth, confirmed at age 12. I'm on my way to heaven." Across the street in another high corner tower people will say, "I went forward as a child, was baptized, and am eternally secure." On the opposite corner a people will tell you, "I was saved by baptism and am kept by good works. This is the only high corner tower that will take you to heaven," and so forth.

All of these high corner towers have taken a part of the gospel, perhaps even a good part, and used it as the whole gospel to capture the hearts of people. This is idolatry. The hearts of the people blindly trust their doctrines rather than being led by the Spirit of God into all truth (John 16:13).

Slogans Replace
the Word of God

Congregations are indoctrinated with slogans and isolated scriptures rather than being instructed in the whole Word of God which would lead them to obedience and holiness. Echoing through the towers you hear: "Christians aren't perfect, just forgiven"; "Everyone sins"; "Once saved, always saved"; "Well after all, nobody's perfect"; "Don't doubt your salvation; I heard you pray the prayer"; "It's easy to be saved; all you have to do is follow me in this prayer."

The religious structures today become an expression of a form of godliness through their traditions, doctrines and rituals, rather than becoming an expression of Jesus (which is true godliness). These structures lead people to make a commitment to their structure rather than to Jesus. The structures then become idols. It does not really matter how the church members live or whether they walk out separate doors because of unforgiveness in their hearts toward other church members. It only matters that they show up for the religious exercises. When this happens in a congregation, a spirit of sleep and darkness covers the multitude. The Spirit of God can have no control in their lives. They are lords of their own lives and live in spiritual darkness.

Jesus said: "... 'This people honors Me with their lips, but their heart is far from Me. But *in vain* do they worship Me, teaching as *doctrines* the precepts (opinions) of men (man-centered religion). Neglecting the commandment of God, you hold to the traditions of men' " (Mark 7:6-8).

If you love fleshly traditions and carnal doctrines, your heart becomes hardened and you resist the true gospel. If Christ has all your heart, you will come to the whole counsel of God's Word.

It is only through the Word showing us the motives of our hearts that we are ever able to turn from sin and walk in righteousness. It is only as the Word divides spirit from soul and flesh that we learn to hear the Holy Spirit speak to us. We can then turn aside from soulish and fleshly religion to walk before the Lord in holiness and purity, putting to death all the deeds of the flesh: "As obedient children, do not be conformed to the former lusts (of the flesh) which were yours in your ignorance, but like the Holy One who called you, be holy yourselves in all your behavior; because it is written, 'You shall be holy, for I am holy' " (I Pet. 1:14-16.)

The Pharisees were blinded to righteousness and holiness because of their religious structures. Those structures led them after carnal traditions and fleshly desires. Therefore they were blinded and could not receive any more light from the Word of God. The Word could have *no place* in them because God did not have their hearts: "... He who is of God hears the words of God; for this reason *you do not hear them, because you are not of God*" (John 8:47).

They were offended and wanted to kill Jesus because He tried to lead them out of darkness with new light. Jesus said: "I am ... a man who has told you the truth, which I heard from God ... You are seeking to kill Me because My word has no place in you" (John 8:40, 37).

It is no different today for people whose hearts have been captured by carnal traditions which lead people after fleshly desires. They will hate everyone who brings new light contrary to their religious structure: "And if our gospel is veiled, it is veiled to those who are perishing, in whose case the god of this world (Satan and the powers of darkness) has blinded the minds of the unbelieving that they may not see the light of the gospel of the glory of Christ ..." (II Cor. 4:3, 4).

The Flesh Nature Loves Darkness

The Word tells us: "And this is the judgment (today) that the light is come into the world, and men loved darkness (flesh) rather than the light (Jesus); for their deeds were evil (selfishness). For everyone who does evil (walks after the flesh) hates the light, and does not come to the light (shrinks back), lest his deeds should be exposed. But he who practices the truth, comes to the light (receives the word), that his deeds may be manifested as having been wrought in God" (John 3:19-21). His ambition is to please the Lord more than anything else.

Every time you read the Word, you make a choice. Either you will continue to love rebellion and walk after the flesh and the ways of Satan, or you will come to the light (obedience) and love the Lord and the ways of God and be perfected in holiness. If you have a stubborn heart, you will shrink back from the Word of God and choose to continue to live in fleshly rebellion.

Motives of Pride and Greed

When there is not genuine repentance, people will try to do the work of God through the strength of the flesh. The flesh nature continues doing inside the church what it always did in the world. Instead of striving to make it to the top in the world, it strives to make it to the top in a religious structure.

Men who attempt to come to Jesus and still love the flesh nature will still have selfish ambition. They will try to have the biggest building, the largest and best choir, the greatest numbers, and the best reputation for building a church. Instead of obedience to the Word of God and holiness, their goal is "nickles, noses, and numbers" to fulfill their selfish ambition. They say, "Come see my church!"

Religious towers are being built today by people who are seeking to make a name for themselves just as the people did when they built the Tower of Babel. They, in almost every instance, are not even aware that they are motivated by pride and greed (the works of the flesh).

Pride (self-love) never makes a name for Jesus. A proud man becomes more proud because he helps God after the strength and works of the flesh. He believes that religious activity is godliness. People in apostasy are unaware of this deception. Loving pride and greed is the very opposite of the purposes of Christ who said: "This is

My commandment that you love one another, just as I have loved you" (John 15:12). Loving pride and greed is to continue loving the character and nature of Satan.

Pride and greed were the idols in the hearts of the false teachers in II Peter 2. If a person loves pride and greed, he will compromise the Word of God and exploit his congregation to fulfill his love for pride and greed. His heart will seek to build a self image and reputation more than the image of Christ. The motive of his heart is selfishness instead of love because he has never truly repented and turned from the sinful flesh nature. His prideful and greedy flesh has simply become religious and now seeks ways to share the glory with God. We repent from pride and greed when we come to follow Jesus.

2

The Nature of Satan
or the Nature of God

This is probably the most important chapter in this book. Plan to move slowly through this chapter in order that you may have clear understanding of how the powers of darkness tempt and attack us through the flesh nature. When Jesus Christ and the Spirit of God control our lives, we overcome the flesh nature in order to be conformed to the image of Jesus. The Spirit of God leads us to overcome the nature of Satan in order that we will have the nature of God and walk in holiness.

We will first see how the cursed nature of Satan came upon everyone in the world and also how we repent and overcome this nature in order to be conformed to the image of Jesus. There will be four very important illustrations which will help to give us light to clearly understand the scriptures which will explain the great falling away today.

The First Adam
Brought the Cursed Nature

In the very beginning, Adam, the first man, was created in the image of God (Gen.1:27). He had total innocence and a pure heart with *no impure motives.* He was holy and blameless. Since God tests the hearts of everyone He has created, Adam was given a choice between the tree of life and the tree of death. On the tree of death were the lust of the flesh, the lust of the eyes, and the boastful pride of life — everything that represents rebellion to God. God told Adam; "...From the tree of the knowledge of good and evil you shall not eat, for in the day that you eat from it *you shall surely die*" (Gen. 2:17).

Then Satan tempted Eve (with a lie) to eat from the tree of death by telling her, *"You surely shall not die"* (another doctrine) (Gen 3:4). So Eve ate from the tree of the lust of the flesh, the lust of the eyes, and the boastful pride of life. Since Adam apparently loved Eve more than he loved God, when Eve gave this fruit to Adam, he ate also.

Because of this sin of Adam, all mankind received a cursed nature, the nature of Satan or the "flesh" nature. Everyone in the world then walked in self-love, self-centeredness and selfishness. They did not love God or their neighbors. They lived for themselves, like Satan.

The Flesh Nature
Is The Nature Of Satan

When man broke fellowship with God, the judgment of God rested on all mankind: "... Through one man (Adam) sin entered into the world, and death through sin, so (the judgment of) death spread to all men because all sinned" (Rom. 5:12).

Today all the world walks in the image and likeness of Satan because they all have this cursed nature. Everyone loves their selfish natures until they see the gospel of Jesus and repent.

The flesh nature and the nature of Satan are the same. Therefore they are in total agreement. When your heart loved this flesh nature, your motives were the same as Satan: selfishness and self-love. Satan controlled your life because your heart loved this selfish and cursed nature. The flesh nature is hostile to God and will not subject itself to the law of God (Rom. 8:7).

The deeds or fruit of the flesh represent the character and nature of Satan. Because this nature is rooted deeply in the hearts of all mankind, their only *motive* will be to satisfy the desires of their flesh and *live for themselves*. The Lord Jesus Christ obviously has to do something about this flesh nature or we would never be able to be obedient to the Spirit of God. This is why the Spirit of God leads us to put to death the deeds of the rebellious flesh (Rom. 8:13, 14; Gal. 5:16, 24). In the new covenant, the Lord Jesus enables us to overcome this flesh nature in order to be conformed to the image of Christ.

In the following illustrations, we will see how we may know the motives of a man's heart by the words which proceed from his mouth. This is called discernment. Jesus has clearly warned us that we will be able to identify the body of Christ or false teachers by the fruit or words of a person's mouth because all words come from a person's heart. It is with the heart that a man believes unto right - eousness or with the heart that he believes unto unright - eousness. Therefore, if we are going to use the scripture to show how the church has fallen away from the faith, it is very important that we understand what the Lord is teaching us about the heart and its fruit.

A form of godliness has clouded these scriptures in such a way that no reference is made to them. However, when we understand these scriptures, we can begin seeing the things that Jesus is warning us about today.

In the first illustration we will see a man of the world before he comes to know the Lord Jesus Christ. The second illustration will be this same man after he has repented and made Jesus Christ Lord. The Spirit of God has led him to overcome the flesh nature. Therefore he now bears the fruit of the Spirit. In the last two illustrations will be men who come to Jesus without true repentance. They do not overcome the flesh but walk in double-mindedness. You will know them by their fruit. Study each illustration carefully and return to these illustrations often as you read the book in order to have a better understanding of the scriptures.

In this first illustration we see the worldly man whose heart loves the fleshly nature of Satan. We can understand the motives of his heart by the words that proceed from his mouth. The evidence of a heart which loves this selfish nature will be the fruit of the flesh. In other words, the fruit of his heart will be words that he speaks from his mouth which are *evidence* that the *nature of Satan and selfishness are controlling his heart:* "For from within, *out of the heart* of men, *proceed* (from the mouth) ... deceit, sensuality, envy, slander, pride and foolishness. All these evil things proceed *from within* (the heart) and defile the man (because all these things are sin)" (Mark 7:21-23).

"For his mouth speaks from that which fills his heart" (Luke 6:45). This man's heart loves the selfish nature of Satan. You will know him by his fruit.

God calls all the words of this flesh nature (cursed nature) sin, because this fruit is the evidence that the heart is in rebellion to God. The works of the flesh are the very opposite of loving your neighbor and loving the nature of God. These deeds of the flesh are the very sins we repent and turn from to follow Jesus Christ: "Their tongue is a deadly arrow; it speaks deceit. With his mouth one speaks peace to his neighbor, but inwardly (in his heart) he sets an ambush for him" (Jer. 9:8).

When anyone loves the flesh nature, he will use and exploit his neighbor because he seeks his own selfish interests. This is why everyone in the world is full of distrust and suspicion toward one another. *People of the world know one another's motives are selfish and deceitful.*

They will never have understanding of their dilemma until they turn to God, their Creator, and hear the gospel of the Lord Jesus Christ. God is the source of all true knowledge and wisdom. God tests the hearts of all mankind by giving them a choice to seek knowledge and wisdom

ROOT: THE FLESH NATURE OF SATAN

(The root is the motive that controls a man's heart.) If a man loves the flesh nature more than he loves God, the selfish motives of the flesh nature will fill his heart.

FRUIT

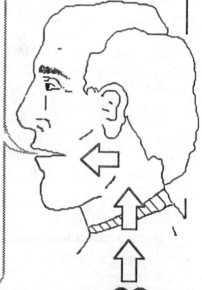

JEALOUSY	STEALING
ENVY	HATRED
ANGER	CRITICAL
WORRY	REBELLION
FEAR	REJECTION
GREED	RETALIATION
MALICE	REVENGE
STEALING	NEGATIVISM
SCOFFING	IMPATIENCE
SLANDER	SARCASM
MURDER	BITTERNESS
IRRITABLE	
STUBBORNNESS	
APPROVAL OF MAN	
UNMERCIFUL	
BOASTFUL	
UNFORGIVENESS	
GRUMBLING	
COVETOUSNESS	

EVIDENCE:
SELFISHNESS

INNER ♥ MAN

Root: Loves the flesh nature of Satan

The motives of a man are rooted in his heart. This heart loves the flesh nature.

from Him or be lord of their own lives, like Satan. Everyone who does not turn from loving this selfish nature is wise in his own eyes.

When anyone loves the flesh nature, Satan will be his master because he will be able to control his heart and life through thoughts and suggestions which fulfill his selfish desires. The powers of darkness will lead him to seek the selfish opportunities of the world because he lives for himself. Since he loves selfishness, the powers of darkness will also begin tearing down all his relationships with suggestions and thoughts of jealousy, distrust, rejection, suspicion and unforgiveness toward his neighbor. He will welcome these thoughts since he seeks his own self interest rather than the interests of his neighbor. He will seek an advantage and be deceitful in all his deeds like his master, Satan, until he has a change of heart. This change of heart is called repentance.

When anyone loves the nature of Satan, he does not love his neighbor. Since God demands that he love his neighbor, every act or word that does not show love for God or for his neighbor is sin and rebellion. God made a provision through the last Adam, Jesus Christ, to restore him to fellowship by taking all of his sins on Him through the cross of Calvary.

He becomes a totally different man when he comes to God in repentance and receives Jesus Christ as his new Master and Lord. The Spirit of God then leads him to be perfected in love. He has seen the gospel. He has seen the judgment and destruction that is on each man who loves and walks in the ways of Satan and the flesh.

He also understands that God is demanding that he love Him with all his heart instead of loving the flesh nature of Satan. Since he now loves the Lord instead of this selfish flesh nature, his motives are changed from selfishness to love. Previously, the root or motive of his heart was to please the selfish desires of the flesh. Now the root (motive)

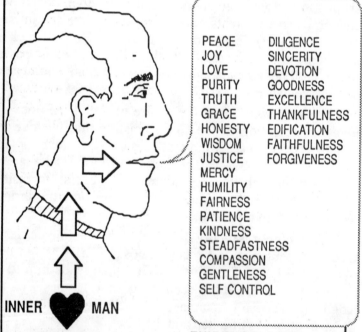

ROOT: THE LORD JESUS CHRIST

(The root is the motive that controls a man's heart.) If a man loves Jesus Christ with all his heart, he will put to death the deeds of the flesh because all of his motives are to please Jesus Christ more than the flesh nature.

FRUIT

PEACE	DILIGENCE
JOY	SINCERITY
LOVE	DEVOTION
PURITY	GOODNESS
TRUTH	EXCELLENCE
GRACE	THANKFULNESS
HONESTY	EDIFICATION
WISDOM	FAITHFULNESS
JUSTICE	FORGIVENESS
MERCY	
HUMILITY	
FAIRNESS	
PATIENCE	
KINDNESS	
STEADFASTNESS	
COMPASSION	
GENTLENESS	
SELF CONTROL	

INNER ♥ MAN

Root: Loves
Jesus Christ
with all his heart

EVIDENCE: *LOVE*

He loves Jesus with all his heart.

of his heart will be to please the Lord Jesus Christ with all of his heart.

Jesus then leads him by His Spirit to overcome the flesh, the world and the devil in order to purify his heart and perfect him in love. The Spirit of God will lead him to put to death the deeds of the rebellious flesh one by one, until he has a pure heart. This is how he overcomes. His mind will be renewed by the Word of God so he will walk and talk like Christ instead of like Satan.

Since he now has the mind of Christ instead of the mind of Satan, he will bear a new kind of fruit. This fruit is the fruit of the Spirit, the fruit of a pure heart — the fruit of love. His heart believes unto righteousness and he walks in holiness.

This man has now been perfected in love and conformed to the image of Jesus Christ. He has a totally new heart and a renewed mind. His heart has been cleansed by God's Word and he now walks and talks like our Lord. He has the mind of Christ and no longer walks according to the flesh.

Paul identifies this body of Christ by saying: "Now those who belong to Jesus Christ have crucified the flesh with its passions and desires" (Gal. 5:24.) We then see that the "...whole law is fulfilled in one word, in the statement, 'You shall love your neighbor as yourself' " (Gal. 5:14).

The Spirit of God leads us to put to death the deeds of the flesh so we will love our neighbor as Christ has loved us).

If someone comes to God and does not repent and turn from pride, he is still walking in rebellion. He is really saying in his heart, "I will not give up pride because I love pride more than I love God."

In the next illustration you will see this man who has a root of pride in his heart. Once established, this root becomes a mighty fortress for the powers of darkness. We will see later in this book how Satan uses pride to deceive the body of Christ.

EVIDENCE: BUILDING A SELF IMAGE

SELF GLORY VANITY RUDE
CONTROL INSENSITIVE SUPERIORITY
SELFISHNESS ARROGANCE SELF LOVE BOASTING
LOOKS DOWN ON OTHERS   SELF JUSTIFICATION
UNSUBMISSIVE   MAKES A NAME FOR SELF
REBELLIOUS   SELF RIGHTEOUS
OVERBEARING   WANTS ATTENTION
SELF AMBITION   ALWAYS RIGHT
MANPLEASER   PRESUMPTUOUS
INSOLENT   SELF INTEREST
CONCEIT   MASTERFUL
UNLOVING   HAUGHTINESS
I, ME, MY   EGO

ROOT: PRIDE

(when you think you're better than others)

If a man has never repented
and turned from pride,
the motives of pride
will fill his heart.

We can see in this illustration how Satan uses pride to build many strongholds of deceit. Pride is the root and symptom of countless other areas of sin. We are to know false teachers by their fruit. As you study this illustration, picture this man as a spiritual leader.

If a person has this root of pride, his *motive* will be to build an image for himself. As he builds a name for Jesus after the strength and works of the flesh, he will deceitfully take part of the glory which belongs to Jesus to fulfill his love for pride and reputation. He will show partiality and exploit his relationships with others in order to fulfill this selfish ambition. He will flatter and deceive others in order to look good and receive the approval of man. Pride always wants to be the center. Pride receives glory from men. Pride holds up his own image. Pride is always right. Pride loves the approval of man rather than the approval of God. Pride will welcome thoughts and suggestions from Satan to exploit and use people to build one's own self image.

Another fortress which is built by Satan in the lives of men is the root of greed. Like pride, greed is also a symptom of numerous strongholds which have their foundation in the root of greed. Greed does not love his neighbor. Greed loves the things of the world. Greed hoards and spends his whole life living for himself and building a fleshly kingdom for himself. Greed acts as if he is going to live forever. He is deceitful and manipulates his neighbor to fulfill his selfish ambition. When anyone loves greed, he is loving the nature of Satan rather than the giving and loving nature of God. In this next illustration, picture a man who loves the selfish ways of greed trying to follow the Lord Jesus Christ.

Can God control the life of a man whose heart loves greed? Can anyone who loves greed truly love his neighbor?

Picture a salesman in the world system whose heart loves greed. He will exaggerate, withhold information, apply pressure, manipulate, and intimidate his neighbor to make a sale to fulfill his lust for greed. He exploits and uses his neighbor because he loves greed and selfishness more

EVIDENCE: SELFISH AMBITION

STRIFE

CHEATING · DECEIT

LYING · CONTROL

PRIDE · FLATTERY

JEALOUSY · DISCONTENT

SELFISHNESS · POSSESSIVE

MATERIAL LUST · COVETOUSNESS

EXAGGERATION · LOVER OF MONEY

MANIPULATION · SELFISH AMBITION

HOARDING · LOVER OF MONEY

STINGY · ENVY

ROOT: GREED

If a man has never repented
and turned from greed,
the motives of (root of) greed
will fill his heart.

than he loves his neighbor. This is why the judgment of God is on the world today. The god of this world, Satan, has trained the world to love greed and get to the top, regardless of who suffers. This is called success by the standards of the fleshly world.

When anyone loves greed, he will love the thoughts and suggestions from the powers of darkness which tell him how to deceitfully manipulate and exploit his neighbor. The same is true for the man in a church who has not repented and still loves greed. He will live and build for himself. This is how the world is in the church today. The man who loves greed does not love his neighbor. Greed hates and uses his neighbor. Of course, what God calls love and what the world calls love, are two very different things.

When anyone does not turn from greed, he will use the things of God to build opportunities for himself and fulfill his lust for greed. Lust of the flesh is when one's heart is drawn to love something else more than he loves the Lord. In this case, he is loving greed more than he loves God. This is idolatry. John warns us: "Do not love the world, nor the *things* in the world. If anyone loves the world (the ways of the world and the things of the world more than God), *the love of the Father is not in him.* For *all* that is in the world, the lust of the flesh, the lust of the eyes, and the boastful pride of life, is not from the Father, but is from the world. And the (fleshly) world is passing away (destroyed) and also its lusts (the desires for other things rather than God); but the *one who does the will of God* (loves God and his neighbor) abides forever" (I John 2:15-17).

The Psalmist described the ones who love pride and greed: "In pride the wicked hotly pursue the afflicted; let them be caught in the plots which they have devised. For the wicked boasts of his heart's desire (pride), and the *greedy man* curses and spurns the Lord. His (greedy) ways prosper at all times; *Thy judgments* are on high, *out of his sight* ... As for all his adversaries (judgment), he snorts at them. He says to himself, 'I shall not be moved; throughout all generations I shall not be in adversity' (thinking he will live forever without judgment). His mouth is full of curses (speaking against his neighbor) and *deceit* and oppression; under his tongue is mischief and wickedness. He says to himself, 'God has forgotten; He has hidden His face; He will never see it' " (Ps. 10:2, 3, 5-7, 11).

When a worldly church still walks after the flesh and loves pride, greed, and selfish ambition, there is no differ-ence between them and the world.

The Psalmist also said "Help, Lord, for the godly man ceases to be, for the faithful (in God's church) disappear from among the sons of men. They speak falsehood to one another; with *flattering lips* and with a *double heart* they speak. The wicked strut about on every side, when vileness (worthlessness) is *exalted* among the sons of men. May the Lord cut off all flattering lips, the tongue that speaks great things; who have said ... Our lips are our own; who is lord over us?" (Ps. 12:1, 2, 8, 3, 4).

Every man in the world walks in the image and likeness of Satan. He does not love nor honor God; neither does he love his neighbor. Each one in the world lives for himself. The strong deceive, manipulate, and "lord it over" the weak. Everyone greedily gathers and hoards for himself, while all around him his neighbor hurts and suffers in need. "... The whole world lies in the power of the evil one" (I John 5:19), because their hearts agree with Satan.

The Powers of Darkness
Control Men Through Thoughts

Satan is the god of this world (I Cor. 4:4). Since the way of Satan and the way of the flesh is the same, the powers of darkness are continually directing the hearts of the people in the world toward selfishness. Because both the people of the world and the worldly people in the church love this selfish nature, Satan uses them as puppets, keeping their minds and hearts occupied with selfish ambition and the things of this present world.

Satan leads the whole world to practice sin and rebellion toward God. The people of the world welcome the thoughts and suggestions from the powers of darkness such as anger, unforgiveness, hate, envy, lust, jealousy, greed, pride and revenge.

Everyone walks and talks like his master, Satan. You will know them by their fruits. However, the Spirit of God leads Christians to take all these selfish thoughts captive that exalt themselves against the Word of God in order that they may walk in loving obedience to Christ. This is how we resist Satan and the flesh.

Satan and the powers of darkness have the whole world seeking success, power, control, beauty, greed, selfish ambition, name and reputation. Everyone deceives his neighbor in order to seek these selfish interests for himself. He seldom considers the needs of his neighbor or his Creator because of his selfish motives.

Therefore, the whole world is under judgment and the wrath of God. The sentence of death rests upon each person in the world. With every act of rebellion toward God and his neighbor, the powers of darkness are able to put chains of bondage on each one as he continues to walk with no hedge of protection from God. With every act against God or his neighbor, the powers of darkness are able to build stronghold upon stronghold, fortress upon fortress, until he is destroyed. This judgment comes upon him because he loves the nature of Satan (to hate his neighbor), rather than the nature of God (to love his neighbor). He walks in spiritual ignorance and spiritual darkness because he does not seek the One who created him with his whole heart.

God permits the heart of every man to be tested. From morning until night, the powers of darkness tempt his heart against his neighbor or entice his heart with things of the world. Satan will remain his master as long as he does not come to receive wisdom and knowledge from God to walk in love. Without the wisdom of God he will remain in ignorance and be destroyed in this spiritual darkness.

Each person in the world spends his entire life living for himself and comparing himself with others: "... But when they measure themselves by themselves and compare themselves by themselves, they are without understanding" (II Cor. 10:12). "And the people who were sitting in (spiritual) darkness saw a great light, to those who were sitting in the land and shadow of *death* (being destroyed), upon them a light (the word of God) dawned ... Jesus began to preach (the gospel) and say, *'repent'* (change your heart) ..." (Matt. 4:16, 17).

The Last Adam Brought Holiness and Righteousness

When man sees the gospel which is light and revelation from God, he will see that death and judgment are upon him. He will also see that his heart is in rebellion to God. The last Adam, Jesus Christ, came to restore every man to walk in justice and righteousness in order that he may be reconciled to God. Each man must repent by changing the direction of his heart and making Jesus Christ his new Master and Lord. He will no longer exploit or use his neighbor. The Spirit of God will then perfect him in the God kind of love which is called holiness, the nature of God.

Jesus was led by the Spirit of God to have his heart tested in the same way Eve was tested. Satan tempted Jesus after the lust of the flesh, the lust of the eyes, and the boastful pride of life. Jesus proved His heart was holy and blameless.

We are also tempted as Jesus was tempted. When we choose the way of the first Adam, walking after the lusts of the flesh, the result is sin and death. If we choose the way of Jesus, we will resist the selfish flesh and the result is sanctification (a pure heart) and holiness: "And just as we have borne the image of the earthy (Adam), we shall also bear the image of heavenly (Jesus)" (I Cor. 15:49.)

Our hearts will either choose the nature of God or the nature of Satan. This is the test for all mankind today.

3

The Law and the Powers of Darkness Today

Deliverance ministries have been springing up in churches all over the country to set people free from the powers of darkness. Pastors by the thousands have come to know there is demonic bondage in their own congregations, in their own lives, and in their own families.

Most do not deal with the problem because, first, they do not understand it; secondly, they are fearful because they don't have the answers; thirdly, they fear it would destroy their theology; and fourthly, they fear their involvement would cause them to lose support, numbers, their reputation, or even their jobs.

So congregations stay in darkness and most deliverance ministries stay very, very busy. Most people who receive freedom do not continue in freedom, but return to the same bondage.

There are some questions about this demonic bondage in the church today. How did this bondage get there? Why is all this happening? Is God trying to tell us something? Obviously, we have missed the truth somewhere. We have to admit that we have never had a proper understanding of the powers of darkness.

I once heard a pastor say, "If the law has been done away with, why do I see the curses of the law shown in

Deuteronomy 28 in my congregation, in my family, and even in my body?" The answer is that our religious traditions have caused us to have a total lack of understanding about the part the law of God plays in the life of a Christian. We certainly need to set the captives free, but we also need to stop and deal with the question, "Why are they there?" After all, the powers of darkness are an enemy who has come "... to steal, and kill, and destroy ..." (John 10:10). They are not blessings.

Something usually happens when anyone offers new light concerning the law — there returns a cry of "legalism." If you are unwilling to learn and unlearn some things about the law, you will never know freedom, or have understanding about the workings of the powers of darkness.

Since this is a very difficult subject, first agree that none of us have all the light. Then agree that if God has given new understanding and light, it will be in the Bible, in balance and context. Do not be like the Pharisees and react to the first statement you hear which is contrary to your traditions. If we are in some darkness in our religious traditions, let's be willing to be led out of this darkness by the Word of God. But let's first admit that we have obviously missed it somewhere.

Stay with the scriptures throughout this chapter and book, even though at first they may seem rather disturbing to you. Most everything will fit together before we finish. In addition, remember that the truth always comes against anything we have learned wrong. If we love the Lord more than any religious traditions, we can then unlearn anything we have learned wrong. Then the Lord can lead us out of spiritual darkness.

What Does
The Law Say Today?

When the law is mentioned to many people, they think only of the rituals which were done away with when Jesus came to fulfill the law. The rituals did pass away, but the law still stands today. Jesus said, "Do not think that I came to abolish the Law ... I did not come to abolish, but to fulfill" (Matt. 5:17).

Since Jesus came to fulfill the law, we need to first know what the law is really saying. Jesus answered this in Matthew 22:37-40: "... *You shall love the Lord your God with all your heart,* and with all your soul, and with all your mind. This is the great and foremost commandment. The second is like it, *You shall love your neighbor as yourself.* On these two commandments depend the *WHOLE LAW* ..."

What the law is really saying is that if you do these two things, love the Lord with all your heart and love your neighbor as yourself, you have fulfilled the law and you are no longer a law breaker. But this is impossible without Christ because of our bondage to the selfish flesh nature.

Since Jesus did not abolish the law, then what does the law do today? The law stands today to bring judgment upon all sin. The law brings the wrath of God (Rom. 4:15). The law brings a curse (Gal. 3:13). The law is a ministry of death (II Cor. 3:7), and the law is a ministry of condemnation (II Cor. 3:9). All of these things come upon all law breakers.

Who are the law breakers? They are those who do not walk in love because their minds are set upon the nature of Satan, the flesh. Since our minds are set upon the things our hearts love, then "... the mind (which is) set on the *flesh* is hostile toward God; *for it does not subject itself to the law of God* (which commands us to walk in love) ..." (Rom. 8:7). Therefore, anyone who loves the flesh nature refuses to love the Lord with all his heart and his neighbor as himself. He chooses to walk in the image of Satan.

Jesus was asked "... *'What good thing shall I DO that I may obtain eternal life?'* And He said to him, ... 'if you wish to enter into (eternal) life, keep the commandments.' He said to Him, 'Which ones?' And Jesus said, '... You shall not steal; you shall not bear false witness; honor your father and

mother; and *you shall love your neighbor as yourself* "
(Matt. 19:16-19).

Obviously, if someone loves his neighbor as himself,
he will not murder his neighbor, he will not commit
adultery, he will not steal, or bear false witness against his
neighbor. Anyone who still loves the flesh nature of Satan
refuses to obey God's law. The law stands in judgment
today against all this rebellion. Paul said, "... For not the
hearers of the Law are just before God, but *the doers of the
Law will be justified*" (Rom. 2:13).

When we understand that God is commanding us to
walk in this love or be destroyed, then we can see the
dilemma of Paul in Romans 7. We find ourselves in exactly
the same place as Paul. Like Paul, we know that through our
efforts alone it is impossible to keep the law. We cannot
walk in this kind of love when we are in bondage to the
selfish flesh nature.

Paul said, "For we know that the Law is spiritual; *but I
am of flesh, sold into bondage to sin* ... for I am not
practicing what I would like to do, but I am doing the very
thing I hate. For I know that nothing good dwells in me, that
is, *in my flesh*; for the wishing is present in me, but the
doing of the good is not ... I *practice* the very evil (the deeds
of the flesh) that I do not wish. I find then the principle that
evil is present in me, the one who wishes to do good. For I
joyfully concur with the law of God (to walk in love) in the
inner man, but I see a different law (to hate my neighbor) in
the members of my (fleshly) body ... making me a prisoner
of the law of sin ... So then, on the one hand I myself with
my mind am serving the law of God, but on the other, with
my flesh the law of sin (double-mindedness)" (Rom. 7:14,
15, 18, 19, 21-23, 25).

Paul saw that he was under the judgment, wrath, curse,
death and condemnation of the law, because he saw that he
could not himself walk in the love which the law required.
Paul said, "... For if a law had been given which was able to
impart (eternal) life, then righteousness would indeed have

been based on the law" (Gal. 3:21). In other words, if we could have attained righteousness by our efforts alone to overcome the flesh and fulfill the requirements of the law, then Jesus would never have needed to go to the cross. Paul added, "... If righteousness comes through the law, then Christ died needlessly" (Gal. 2:21).

However, this does not explain away the fact that *we are still* commanded to love our neighbor as ourselves. Jesus came to fulfill the law by perfecting this God-kind of love in us. This is how we are reconciled back to God. A form of godliness has explained this love away today by saying it is impossible to walk in the kind of love required by the law. This is true if you are led by a doctrine that does not conform you to godliness, instead of being led by the Spirit of God.

When we are led by the Spirit of God we are not under the judgment of the law because we are fulfilling the law by walking in love. When we walk after the flesh, we defraud and take advantage of our neighbor. This is sin and this breaks God's law. Those who sin by walking after the flesh do not have a hedge of protection against the powers of darkness. Therefore, the powers of darkness bring the judgment, wrath and curse of the law on all those who walk after the works of the flesh.

Jesus Explained The Love That Fulfills The Law

Jesus explained to His disciples the God-kind of love they were commanded to walk in to fulfill the requirements of the law. "And turning His gaze on His disciples, He began to say ... Love your enemies, do good to those who hate you ... whoever takes away what is yours, do not demand it back. And just as you want people to treat you, treat them in the same way ... if you love those who love you, what credit is that to you? For even sinners (who walk after the flesh) love those who love them. But love your enemies, and do good, and lend ... and *YOU WILL BE*

SONS OF THE MOST HIGH; (and be like your Father who) ... is kind to ungrateful and evil men. Be merciful (toward others), just as your Father is merciful' " (Luke 6:20, 27, 30-32, 35, 36).

You manifest the nature of God when you love your neighbor as yourself. Every time the disciples obeyed these commandments, they proved they were not of this world.

This message is to all the disciples of the Lord Jesus Christ, to the body of Christ. The reason these scriptures sound like a foreign language to most people today is because of the fact that they will not fit into today's carnal doctrines. These doctrines do not teach people to fulfill the law nor do they conform them to godliness to walk in the love God demands. True disciples receive discipline in order to walk in this love. This is the God-kind of love that Jesus perfects in the body of Christ to fulfill the law.

Jesus confirmed the God-kind of love that we are to walk in today by saying, "This is My commandment, that you love one another, *JUST AS I HAVE LOVED YOU ...* that one lay down his life (in the flesh) for his friends" (John 15:12, 13). We must be obedient to the Spirit of God and the Word of God in order to be perfected in God's love. "The one who says, 'I have come to know Him,' and does not keep His commandments, is a liar, and the truth is not in him ... *by this we know that we have come to know Him, if we keep His commandments"* (I John 2:4, 3). "... Whoever keeps His word, in him the love of God has truly been perfected ... the one who says he abides (or continues) in Him ought himself to *walk in the same manner as He walked"* (I John 2:5, 6).

"We know (the God kind of) love by this, that He laid down His life for us; and we ought to lay down our lives (in the selfish flesh) for the brethren" (I John 3:16). Jesus described the body of Christ by saying, "... Whoever wishes to become great among you shall be your servant,

and whoever wishes to be first among you shall be your slave (love); just as the Son of Man did not come to be served (selfishness), but to serve (love)" ... (Matt. 20:26-28). This is the walk of love that fulfills the law.

We must understand that the gospel of the Lord Jesus Christ is in agreement with the law which says, "You shall love your neighbor as yourself." Jesus referred to this law when He was asked about eternal life. "... Teacher, what shall I do to inherit *eternal life?*" Jesus replied, "... 'What is written in the *Law?*' ... And he answered and said, *'You shall love the Lord your God with all your heart,* and with all your soul, and with all your strength, and with all your mind; and your neighbor as yourself.' And He (Jesus) said to him, *'You have answered correctly; do this; and you will live (eternally)'* " (Luke 10:25-28).

Jesus continued to describe the love we are to walk in, "But I say to you, do not resist him who is evil; but whoever slaps you on your right cheek, turn to him the other also. And if anyone wants to sue you, and take your shirt, let him have your coat also. And whoever shall force you to go one mile, go with him two. Give to him who asks of you, and do not turn away from him who wants to borrow from you. ... Love your enemies, and pray for those who persecute you in order that you may be sons of your Father who is in heaven: ... For if you love those who love you, what reward have you? ... And if you greet your brothers only, what do you do more than others? Do not even the Gentiles (or the world) do the same?" Jesus commanded, "Therefore you are to be perfect, as your heavenly Father is perfect" (Matt. 5:39-42, 44-48). This is the gospel which brought such opposition to Jesus and His disciples. It has not changed.

Jesus was telling the disciples about the *blessings* that would come on those who walk in His love to fulfill the law. He continued to describe this God-kind of love and blessings by saying: "Blessed are those who mourn ... Blessed are the gentle ... Blessed are the merciful ... Blessed are the pure in heart ... Blessed are the peacemakers ...

Blessed are those who have been persecuted ..." Jesus also told the disciples: "You are the light of the world ... Let your light shine before men in such a way that they may see your good works (the nature of God), and glorify your Father who is in heaven" (Matt. 5:4, 5, 7-19, 14, 16).

Jesus explained in the next verse that this was the kind of love which fulfills the law. He said, "... I did not come to abolish (the judgment of) the law, but to fulfill (the law in you as you walk in love)" (Matt. 5:17).

The Judgment Of The Law

God is the Creator of all civilization. He has demanded His creation to walk in justice and righteousness. For this reason God has established laws and judgments, blessings and curses, on all mankind, according to their deeds. God's law demands that we love our neighbor as ourself. God blesses everyone who fulfills this law. However, the law judges every deed contrary to His commandments.

The same judgment is on the worldly people who are in the church today. When someone walks in a form of godliness, he walks just like the world. Since he has a false security, he is blinded and unaware of God's requirement to walk in this love. He is walking in the stubbornness of his heart as he walks in sin without repentance. "For if we go on sinning willfully after receiving the knowledge of the truth, there no longer remains a sacrifice for sins, but a *certain terrifying expectation* of judgment ..." (Heb. 10:26, 27).

"Therefore, be imitators of God, as beloved children; and walk in love, just as Christ also loved you ... But do not let immorality or any impurity or greed even be named among you, as is proper among *saints* (the church)" (Eph. 5:1-3). These scriptures explain the God-kind of love that we are to walk in to escape the judgment and curse of the law. When you lay down your selfish flesh nature, you will love your neighbor as yourself. Remember that "We know love by this, that He laid down His life for us; and we ought to lay down our lives for the brethren" (I John 3:16).

The Powers Of Darkness Draw Us Away From The Faith Walk

We are now understanding the warfare of a Christian with the powers of darkness. The powers of darkness tempt every Christian to walk after the lusts of the flesh and hate his neighbor so they can carry him away from the faith. (Faith is being led by the Spirit of God to be perfected in the nature of God). With these temptations the powers of darkness try to prevent us from being perfected in love for our neighbor. The powers of darkness continually tempt your mind with thoughts of anger, hate, selfishness, resentment, criticism, fault-finding, unforgiveness, etc., etc. These thoughts are the very opposite of love and they exalt themselves against the Word of God. These are the schemes of the devil.

These are the thoughts we are commanded to take "... captive to the obedience of Christ, and we are ready to punish all disobedience, when your obedience is complete" (II Cor. 10:5, 6).

This is why we are warned to "Put on the full armor of God, that you may be able to stand firm against the schemes of the devil. ... In addition to all (or above all), taking up the shield of faith with which you will be able to *EXTINGUISH ALL THE FLAMING MISSILES (fleshly temptations)* of the evil one" (Eph. 6:11, 16).

In Luke 4:1-14, Jesus shows us how He resisted every temptation of the powers of darkness by standing on the Word of God. The Word is our shield of faith. We stand on the Word because we love Jesus more than we love the flesh. Through these temptations Jesus proved Himself holy, as we are to prove ourselves holy.

If we love the flesh more than we love Jesus, we will welcome these thoughts of Satan because these suggestions make an opportunity to fulfill selfishness. But since, as disciples of Jesus, we love Jesus more than any selfishness, we no longer walk in pride, greed, unforgiveness, resentment, criticism, because we are being perfected in the nature of God. When we are reviled and attacked by others, we bless. We no longer war according to the flesh by reacting in anger, hate, slander, revenge. We know that God's laws take care of all revenge.

So we are "... not returning evil for evil, or insult for insult, but giving a blessing instead" (I Pet. 3:9). This is the God-kind of love. "For though we (still) walk in the flesh, we do not war (any longer) according to the flesh, (we no longer strike back at our neighbor) ... we are destroying speculations and every lofty thing (thoughts and schemes of Satan) raised up against the knowledge of God, and *we are taking every thought captive to the* obedience of Christ (gospel)" (II Cor. 10:3-5). This is how we overcome the flesh and the devil to be perfected in love. "And by this we know that we have come to know Him if we keep His commandments" (I John 2:3). We have already seen, "The one who says, 'I have come to know Him'; and does not keep His commandments, is a liar, and the truth is not in Him; but *whoever keeps His word, in him the LOVE OF GOD has truly been PERFECTED. By this* we know that we are in Him *(IN CHRIST)"* (I John 2:4, 5).

The Wrath Of God Comes Against The Deeds Of The Flesh

Paul said, "Set your mind on the things above, not on the things that are on the earth. For you have *died* (to the flesh) and your life is hidden with Christ in God. Therefore consider the members of your earthly body as dead to immorality, impurity, passion, evil desire and greed, which amounts to idolatry (when you practice these things and do not give them up, this is idolatry). For it is on account of these things that the wrath of God will come (the judgment of the Law), and in them you also *once walked*, when you *were* living in them. But *now* you also, *PUT THEM ALL ASIDE:* anger, wrath, malice, slander, and abusive speech from your mouth ... since you laid aside the old self (flesh) with its evil practices, and have put on the new self (the love of Christ in order to love your neighbor as Christ has loved you) ... according to the image of the One who created Him" (Col. 3:2, 3, 5-10).

Powers Of Darkness Carry Out The Curse Of The Law

When you do any act of the flesh which defrauds your neighbor it is sin. Then the hedge comes down and the powers of darkness can then move in to attack. But when you love your neighbor, you are fulfilling the law and are protected by God. "If, however, you are fulfilling the royal law, according to the Scripture, 'You shall love your neighbor as yourself,' you are doing well *(blessed and protected by the hedge of God)*. But if you show partiality (your motives are fleshly and deceitful by loving one person and not loving another), you are committing sin and convicted of the law as transgressors (and the hedge is removed). *SO SPEAK* and *SO ACT* as those who are to be *JUDGED* by the law of liberty. *For judgment* (by *the law) will be merciless to the one who has shown no mercy (love);* mercy triumphs over judgment (of the law)" (James 2:8, 9, 12, 13).

Since the law commands us to love our neighbor, every act of the selfish flesh lowers the hedge on us to the powers of darkness because the flesh causes one to hate his neighbor. For example, the scripture says, "Be merciful, just as your Father is merciful (walking in love). And do not judge and you will not be judged; and do not condemn, and you will not be condemned; pardon, and you will be pardoned ... For by your standard of measure it will be measured to you in return" (Luke 6:36-38).

If we do not seek the good of our neighbor, we will bear the wrong fruit of anger, hate and slander which is sin. When we speak against our neighbor, the hedge is lowered and we are cut down by the powers of darkness because God removes His protection. "And it will be in the day when the Lord gives you rest from your pain and turmoil ... in which you have been enslaved, that you will take up this taunt against the king of Babylon (Satan), and say, 'How the oppressor has ceased, and how fury has ceased! The Lord has broken the staff of the wicked ... which used to strike the peoples in fury with unceasing strokes, which subdued the nations in anger with unrestrained persecution (this is happening right now) ... Since you were laid low (this will happen at a later time), no *tree cutter* comes up against us' " (Isa. 14:3-6, 8).

Satan is the king of Babylon who brings the destruction when the hedge is down. Satan and the powers of darkness are the "tree cutters." When we overcome the flesh, we overcome the destruction of Satan.

At the present time these powers of darkness are at work cutting down and destroying all those whose hearts refuse to be conformed to the nature of God. Our hearts are tested today, just as the first Adam and Eve were tested. "Let me sing now for my well-beloved a song of My beloved concerning His vineyard. My well-beloved had a vineyard on a fertile hill. And He dug it all around ... and planted it with the choicest vine. ... Then He expected it to produce good grapes (the good fruit of love), but it produced only worthless ones (the fruit of the flesh) ... Why, when I expected it to produce good grapes did it produce worthless ones? So now let Me tell you what I am going to do to My vineyard: I will remove its hedge and it will be consumed ..." (Isa. 5:1, 2, 4, 5).

The hedge is down on all those who do not bear the fruit of love toward their neighbor and they are being consumed by the powers of darkness. There is no deliverance or protection for those who refuse to overcome the flesh and walk in covenant with the Lord Jesus Christ to be perfected in love. Our hearts will either love the nature of Satan and the flesh, or our hearts will love the nature of God. This is how we will know a tree by its fruit. "Even so, every good tree bears good fruit (of the Spirit, love); but the bad tree bears bad fruit (of the flesh, hate). A good tree cannot produce bad fruit (of hate), nor can a bad tree produce good fruit (which is the God-kind of love). *Every tree that does not bear good fruit (love) is cut down* (by the powers of darkness) *and thrown into the fire* (because they break God's law when they do not walk in love). So then, you will know them by their fruits" (Matt. 7:14-20).

If we receive the blessings of God by loving our neighbor, then we also receive judgment from God when we choose to defraud our neighbor. If we choose to judge our neighbor instead of loving him, we receive judgment. When we choose to condemn our neighbor instead of loving him, we receive condemnation. If we will not pardon, God will not pardon us. In every case, the hedge comes down and the powers of darkness become instruments of judgment and condemnation. God deals with us according to our conduct toward others — "who will render to every man according to his deeds," (Rom. 2:6). So by your standard of measure toward your neighbors, God measures it in return to you. This is the law of God today.

Curses Prevail
Because The Law Has Been Lost

"Now the end is upon you, and I shall send My anger against you; I shall judge you according to your ways, and I shall bring all your abominations upon you. For My eye will have no pity on you, nor shall I spare you, *but I shall bring your ways upon you* ... and spend My anger against you, *judge you according to your ways, and bring on you all your abominations* ... I will repay *you according to your ways* ...

They have blown the trumpet (warning of judgment) and made everything ready, but no one is going to the battle; for My wrath is against all their multitude. Therefore, I shall bring the worst of the nations (powers of darkness) and they will possess their houses (bodies). I shall also make the pride of the strong ones (after the flesh) cease, and their holy places will be profaned (by the powers of darkness) ... They will seek a vision from a prophet, but THE LAW WILL BE LOST from the priest and from the elders ... *According to their conduct I shall deal with them, and by their judgments I shall judge them.* And they will know that I am the Lord" (Ezek. 7:3, 4, 8, 9, 14, 24, 26, 27).

Ezekiel was talking about today. The law has been lost to us today, as it was lost in the days of Nehemiah. We would have understanding about the fear of the Lord if the law had not been lost.

"Come, you children, listen to Me; I will teach you the fear of the Lord. Who is the man who desires life, and *loves length of days?* ... Keep your tongue from (speaking) evil (against your neighbor), and keep your lips from speaking deceit. Depart from evil, and do good; seek peace (a hedge of protection from God), and pursue it. The eyes of the Lord are toward the righteous ... (but) the face of the Lord is against evildoers, to cut off (destroy) the memory of them from the earth" (Ps. 34:11-16).

Everyone who loves the flesh nature walks in rebellion to God's commandment to walk in love. God has set up His laws in this world to punish and destroy those who love the flesh nature of Satan more than they love the nature of God. Since God has set up punishment for this rebellion, there has to be a law.

If there is a law, there has to be a court. If there is a court, there has to be a judge. The judge of God's court of law is God. Since there is a judge and a court of law, then there must be officers and a prison. The powers of darkness are the officers and their bondage is the prison. The powers of darkness build strongholds and fortresses to destroy everyone in the world who walks in rebellion to God's law. Only those who are fulfilling the law are protected by God.

After Jesus said, "Do not think that I came to abolish the (judgment of the) Law ..." (Matt. 5:17), He began describing the judgment and curses of the Law. "You have heard that the ancients were told, 'You shall not commit murder,' and 'Whoever commits murder shall be liable to the court.' But I say to you that every one who is angry with his brother shall be guilty before the *court* ... Make friends quickly with your *opponent at law* (someone you have wronged) ... in order that your opponent may not deliver you to the *judge* (God), and the *judge* to the *officer* (hedge removed for the powers of darkness), and you be thrown into prison (bondage). ... You shall not come out of there until you have paid the last cent (by repenting and making everything right with your neighbor)" (Matt. 5:21, 22, 25, 26). The law of God has commanded us to love our neighbor as ourself. Jesus described this love for us, then commanded that we "... are to be perfect as your heavenly Father is perfect" (Matt. 5:48).

God says He does all the judging. His laws take care of all vengeance. We are then commanded to do one thing, *walk in love*. We do not speak one word against our neighbor. When we speak against our neighbor, we are taking the place of God and becoming the judge. When we do this, the law judges us. "... If anyone does not stumble in what he says, *he is a perfect man*, able to bridle the whole body as well ... with it (the tongue) we bless our Lord and Father; and with it we curse men ... from the same mouth come both blessing and cursing. My brethren, these things ought not to be this way. This wisdom is ... earthly (as the world speaks), natural (from the flesh nature), and demonic" (James 3:2, 9, 10, 15).

James said "... Cleanse your hands, you sinners; and *purify your hearts, you double-minded* ... Do not speak against one another, brethren. He who speaks (curses) against a brother ... speaks against the law, and judges the law; but if you judge the law, you are not a doer of the law, but a judge of it. *There is only one Lawgiver and Judge, the One who is able to SAVE and to DESTROY ...*"(James 4:8, 11, 12). At this point, you should begin to see that we have been overlooking some essential truths in the scriptures.

The law came through Moses 430 years after God gave the promise to Abraham and made covenant with him. Why was the law needed? It was added because of the transgressions of the people (Gal. 3:19). God spoke to His people in Deuteronomy 28 and told them He would bless them if they obeyed His law, but He would put curses on them and their households if they did not obey the law. This law pronounced a curse of judgment and destruction upon all those who would not walk in love and obedience to God.

Jesus did not come to abolish this judgment. The law and its judgment still stand today against all the works of the flesh which break God's commandments. All of God's commandments tell us that we must walk in love or receive judgment.

Jesus Came To Perfect God's Love In Men

Are we then really expected to love our neighbor as ourselves? The problem today is that the church people do not really love one another. What God calls love and what the church, which walks in a form of godliness, calls love are two different things. *The commandments of Jesus totally agree with the commandments of the law.* Jesus still commands us to love our neighbor as ourselves in order to fulfill the law. Those who walk after a form of godliness cannot fulfill the law. Jesus came to the world to perfect the love in us which fulfills the law. "And this commandment we have from Him, that the one who loves God should love his brother also" (I John 4:21). "By this we know that we love the children of God, when we love God and observe

His commandments. *For this is the love of God*, that we keep His commandments ..." (I John 5:2, 3). These scriptures are sobering to those who have fallen away from the faith to a form of godliness. What part of us wants to resist walking in love? Could it be that we still love the nature of Satan?

"And you *were dead* in your trespasses and sins, in which you *FORMERLY WALKED* according to the course of the world (you walked and talked like the world), according to the *prince of the power of the air*, of the *(demon) spirit* that is *NOW* working *IN* the sons of disobedience (those who walk after the flesh nature). Among them we too all *formerly lived* in the *lusts of our flesh*, indulging the *desires of the flesh* and of the mind, and *were by nature* (of Satan) *children of wrath* (under judgment) ..." (Eph. 2:1-3).

The Flesh Nature
Must Be Put To Death

"That, in reference to your *former manner of life*, you *lay aside the old (fleshly) self*, which is being corrupted in accordance with the *lusts of deceit*, and that you be renewed in the spirit of your mind (to walk and talk like Christ), and put on the new self (love), which (is) in the likeness of God ... in righteousness and holiness of the truth" (Eph. 4:22-24). The purpose of the cross of Jesus was not that we should continue to live in sin, but that we should die to sin. "And He Himself bore our sins in His body on the cross, that we might *die to sin* and *live to righteousness* ..." (I Pet. 2:24). Righteousness is walking right in God's eyes by obeying His commandments.

When we love the flesh, we have our minds set on earthly things. When we love Jesus with all our hearts, we lay down our (fleshly) lives on this earth, because our minds (interests) are set on things above.

Jesus explained how we lay down our lives in John
12:24, 25: "... Unless a grain of wheat falls into the earth
and *dies*, it remains by itself alone; but if it dies, it bears
much fruit (love). *He who loves his (fleshly) life loses it*
(judgment of the law); and he who hates his (fleshly) life in
this world shall keep it to life eternal." This is how we
overcome the powers of darkness. If you have laid down
your life in this world, the powers of darkness have nothing
with which to tempt you. Jesus said, "... For the ruler of this
world is coming, and he has nothing in Me (My flesh)"
(John 14:30). "And they overcame him (the devil) because
of the blood of the Lamb ... and they did not love their
(fleshly) life even unto death" (Rev. 12:11).

How The Powers Of Darkness
Build Strongholds And Destroy Us

God avenges, through His law, every act and word we
speak against our brother. "Either make the tree good, and
its fruit good; or make the tree bad, and its fruit bad; for the
tree is known by its fruit ... How can you, being evil, speak
what is good? For the mouth speaks out of that which fills
the heart. The good man out of his good treasure (the Word
of God hidden in his heart) brings forth what is good (love);
and the evil man out of his evil treasure (the suggestions of
the devil) brings forth what is evil (hate). And I say to you,
that every *careless word* that men shall speak, they shall
render account for it in the day of judgment (we are living
in the day of judgment now). For by your words you shall
be justified (judged righteous), and by your words you shall
be condemned (judged by the law)" (Matt. 12:33-37).

The *mature man* takes every thought captive to the
obedience of Christ "... who *because of practice* have
their senses trained to *discern good and evil*" (Heb.
5:14). The Lord was our example. Our Lord Jesus "...
learned obedience from the things which He suffered.

And having been made perfect, He became to all those who *obey Him* the source of eternal salvation" (Heb. 5:8, 9).

The powers of darkness work at destroying all relationships. They try to keep our minds full of suspicion, unforgiveness, distrust, anger and so forth toward our neighbor. It is essential to stop these thoughts while they are still in our minds so that their evil suggestions (evil treasures) will not get into our hearts. Their goal for getting their suggestions into our hearts is to carry us away from the walk of love by causing us to speak against our neighbor. This is sin and we break the law by not loving our neighbor. "But each one is *TEMPTED* when he is *CARRIED AWAY* (FROM THE FAITH) and *ENTICED* by his own *LUST* (OF THE FLESH). Then when lust has conceived (you welcome the thoughts of the flesh), it gives birth to sin; and when sin is accomplished (this evil enters into your heart and you speak this evil from your mouth), it brings forth DEATH (because God's law is broken)" (James 1:14, 15).

Then the hedge comes down and the powers of darkness can attack us. We immediately lose our peace. If we do not repent, they continue to build other strongholds in our lives which eventually bring death. Strongholds move in when you are a transgressor of the law.

"Do not be *deceived, my beloved brethren* (church) ... But let everyone be quick to hear, *slow to speak and slow to anger*" (James 1:16, 19). Those who speak love from a pure heart do not break God's law. A pure heart is a heart which no longer loves the flesh. In fact, a pure heart hates every act of the flesh. This is the mature man of God.

How Satan Builds
A Stronghold In Us

We will see an example of how Satan builds a stronghold in us. Before Jesus became Lord of your whole heart, you walked after the deeds of the flesh. One of those deeds was unforgiveness. When you came to Jesus, you repented of unforgiveness in order to purify your heart and love your neighbor. One of the schemes of the powers of darkness is to cause you to once again walk in unforgiveness, so they can build strongholds in you.

Paul warned the Corinthians about this scheme of Satan: "But whom you forgive anything, I forgive also ... *in order that no advantage be taken of us by Satan; for we are not ignorant of his SCHEMES*" (II Cor. 2:10, 11).

We will see how Satan builds in us the stronghold of unforgiveness.

Peter was asking the Lord Jesus about forgiveness. "... 'Lord, how often shall my brother sin against me and I forgive him? Up to seven times?' Jesus said to him, 'I do not say to you, up to seven times, but up to seventy times seven' " (Matt. 18:21, 22).

Jesus was replying, in effect, that you always forgive.

Jesus then gave a parable to show the judgment of God upon unforgiveness.

Jesus explained, "For *this reason* the *kingdom of heaven* may be compared to a certain king (Jesus) who wished to settle accounts with his slaves. And when he had begun to settle them, there was brought to him one who owed him ten thousand talents. But since he did not have the means to repay, his lord commanded him to be sold, along with his wife and children and all that he had, and repayment to be made. The slave therefore falling down, prostrated (and humbled) himself before him, saying, 'Have patience with me, I will repay everything.' And the Lord of that slave felt compassion and *released him* and *forgave him the debt*" (Matt. 18:23-27).

This is a picture of us coming to the Lord Jesus Christ for forgiveness from our sin.

We next see what happened to this slave after he was released and forgiven. "... That slave went out and found one of his fellow slaves who owed him a hundred *denarii;*

and he seized him and began to choke him, saying, 'Pay back what you owe.' So his fellow slave fell down and began to entreat him, saying, 'Have patience with me and I will repay you.' He was unwilling, however, but went and threw him in prison ... Then summoning him, his lord said to him, '*You wicked slave*, I forgave you all that debt because you entreated me. Should you not also have had mercy (love) on your fellow slave, even as I have had mercy on you?' " (Matt. 18:28-30, 32, 33). The Lord had forgiven this slave, but he would not forgive his fellow slave.

We now see God's judgment on anyone who defrauds his neighbor and breaks God's law of love by walking in unforgiveness. This judgment brings God's wrath, which lowers the hedge and turns the slave over to the powers of darkness. "And his lord, moved with *anger*, handed him over to the *TORTURERS* (the powers of darkness) until he should repay all that was owed him. *SO SHALL MY HEAVENLY FATHER ALSO DO TO YOU, if each of you does not forgive his brother FROM YOUR HEART*" (Matt. 18:34, 35). If this person continues to walk after the flesh in unforgiveness without repentance, the powers of darkness will continue to build other strongholds until he is destroyed.

"Do nothing from selfishness ... but with humility of mind let each of you regard one another as more important than himself" (Phil. 2:3). "Let this (same) mind be in you, which was also in Christ Jesus ..." (Phil. 2:4 KJV).

If we walk with the mind of Christ, we walk in love and have peace because we are protected by God. If we walk with our mind set on the works of the flesh, we have the mind of Satan. The hedge will continually come down because of these works until the powers of darkness bring death.

This is why Romans 8:13 says, *"For if you are living according to the flesh, you must die;* but if (you are being led) by the Spirit (to walk in love) *you are putting to death the deeds of the body (flesh), you will live.* For all who are being *led by the Spirit* of God, these are the *sons of God*"

(Rom. 8:13, 14). In this scripture you see both life and death, blessings and curses. In order to have the mind of Christ, we must be led by the Spirit to put to death the deeds of the flesh. This is how we purify our hearts. If we choose to continue walking after the deeds of the flesh, the hedge will be down for the powers of darkness who "... come only to steal, and kill, and destroy ..." (John 10:10).

The hedge is down, bringing death on the church today which is choosing to walk after the flesh.

Today the Lord is leading His followers out of this captivity and death. "So it shall be when all of these things have come upon you, the blessing and the curse which I have set before you, and you call them to mind in all the nations where the Lord your God has banished you, and you return to the Lord your God and *OBEY Him with all your heart* and soul according to all that I command you today, you and your sons, then the Lord your God will *restore you from captivity,* and have compassion on you, and will *gather you again from all the peoples* where the Lord your God has scattered you" (Deut. 30:1-3).

Love Your Neighbor To Fulfill The Law

God's law to love your neighbor stood then as it does now: "You shall do no injustice in judgment; you shall not be partial to the poor nor defer to the great, but you are to judge your neighbor fairly. You shall not go about as a slanderer among your people, and you are not to act against the life of your neighbor; I am the Lord. You shall not hate your fellow countryman in your heart; you may surely reprove your neighbor, but shall not incur sin because of him. You shall not take vengeance, nor bear any grudge against the sons of your people, *but you shall love your neighbor as yourself;* I am the Lord. You are to keep My statutes ..." (Lev. 19:15-19).

But the church has not kept God's law just as Israel did not keep God's law. Instead, like Israel, everyone has been doing what seems right to him. "You shall not do at all what we are doing here today, every man doing whatever is right in his own eyes (after the flesh); for you have not as yet come to the resting place (of peace) and the inheritance which the Lord your God is giving you. When you cross the Jordan and live in the land (of peace) which the Lord your God is giving you to inherit, and He gives you rest from all your enemies around you, so that you live in security" (Deut. 12:8-10).

Those who desire to walk with God must stop following their flesh and submit to God's holy walk: "Since the Lord your God walks in the midst of your camp to deliver you and to defeat your enemies before you, therefore your camp must be holy; and He must not see anything indecent among you lest He turn away from you" (Deut. 23:14).

Jesus leads us by His Spirit to put to death the deeds of all fleshly rebellion so that we may fulfill the law and be holy. If we do not resist and put to death the deeds of the flesh, we will continue to have a mind like Satan because the nature of Satan and the ways of the flesh are the same. Putting to death the flesh is the only way we can have a pure heart and be renewed to have the mind of Christ. This is the walk of holiness "... *Walk by the Spirit, and you will not carry out the desires* of the flesh" (Gal. 5:16).

This is the church of Jesus Christ, because "... *if you are led by the Spirit, you are not (any longer) under the (judgment of the) law*" (Gal. 5:18). If you are led by the Spirit, your mind is no longer set on the things of the flesh, but the things of the Spirit. You are no longer under judgment because you no longer break the law. God's presence is in the midst of you to protect, deliver and defeat your enemies.

The result is God's hedge which brings peace: "For the mind set on the flesh is (a walk of) death, ... because *the* mind set on the (things of the) flesh is hostile toward God; for it *does not subject itself to the law of God*, for it is not even able to do so" (Rom. 8:6, 7). Everyone in the world who does not walk in love and obey God's law is destroyed by the powers of darkness. It is a slow death, almost imperceptible, as a moth destroys or as rottenness in a fabric.

The ones who do not receive the Word of God into their hearts to be perfected in love are those who love other things more than they love the Lord. If a person's mind is set on things of the flesh, the powers of darkness will be able to replace the Word in his heart with the desires of the flesh and things of the world. A disciple of Jesus Christ loves the Lord with all his heart and has his mind set totally on things above.

The powers of darkness bring temptation to cause our hearts to love pride, approval of men, greed and things of the world more than we love the Lord. These temptations become roots of all sorts of evil which change our motives from love to selfishness. This prevents us from being perfected in love. When we turn to the ways of Satan, we turn from our faith in Jesus. This is how the powers of darkness take the Word from our hearts and carry us from the faith. The only root and motive in our heart should be to please the Lord.

The parable of the Word best explains how the powers of darkness keep us from being perfected in love and keep us from having understanding. Jesus said to the disciples, "... To you has been given the mystery of the kingdom of God; but those who are outside (the kingdom) get everything in parables, in order that while seeing, they may see and *not perceive;* and while hearing, they may hear and *not understand ...*" (Mark 4:11, 12).

Jesus was saying that only the disciples, the ones who come to Him with all their hearts, will have understanding. Everyone else will not be able to see, hear or understand the mysteries of God today.

Jesus said, "The sower sows the word ... and when they hear, immediately Satan comes and takes away the word which has been sown in them (by turning their hearts to something else) ... These are the ones on whom the seed was sown on the rocky places (a hardened heart), who, when they hear the word, immediately receive it with joy; and they have no firm root (of Jesus) in themselves, but are only temporary; then, when (the fiery trials) of *affliction* or *persecution* arises *because of the word* , immediately they FALL AWAY (from the faith because their hearts turn to things like pride, reputation, greed, treasures of the world, selfishness, and love these things more than the Lord). And (still) others (who resist the Word of God) are the ones who have heard the word ... and the (powers of darkness bring the) worries of the world, and the deceitfulness of riches, and the desires for other things (which they permit to) enter in (their hearts) and choke the word, and it becomes unfruitful" (Mark 4:14-19).

These are examples of the trials that the powers of darkness bring against us to try to stop us from bearing the fruit of love. The powers of darkness try to get our hearts to be set on things of this world by causing us to lust after the riches of this world and the desire for other things so our interest will be to please our flesh rather than to please God and be perfected in love. The opposite of all these is the man of God who is led by the Spirit of God. His motive will be to please the Lord rather than his flesh in everything he does. "And the one on whom (the) seed (Word) was sown on the good soil (repentant heart), this is the man who hears the word and understands it; who indeed *bears* (the) fruit (of love) *AND* brings forth, some a hundredfold, some sixty, and some thirty" (Matt. 13:23).

What You Speak To Others You Will Reap

We experience fear of God as we learn about God's judgment and laws. "Do not be deceived, God is not mocked; for whatever a man sows (he sows either words of love or words of hate toward his neighbor), *this he will also reap.* For the one who *sows to his own flesh* (such as slander, hate, anger, murder, etc.) shall from the flesh *reap corruption* (judgment, because he breaks God's law), *but the one who sows to the Spirit* (sows words of love) *shall from the Spirit reap eternal life"* (Gal. 6:7, 8). This is the walk of salvation, because "... the fruit of the Spirit is (words and acts of) love, joy, peace, patience, kindness, goodness, faithfulness, gentleness, self-control (the God-kind of love); *AGAINST SUCH THINGS THERE IS NO (JUDGMENT OF THE) LAW* (because this is the walk of holiness)" (Gal. 5:22, 23).

We fulfill the law instead of breaking the law when we love our neighbor. This is the fruit of a renewed mind. This is the mature man with a pure heart. He no longer has the mind of Satan; he has the mind of Christ. Therefore, the powers of darkness can get no ground in his life because he is a doer of the law through Jesus Christ: "For not the hearers of the Law are just before God, *but the doers of the Law will be justified"* (Rom. 2:13).

Then how do we put to death the deeds of the flesh? By no longer warring with our neighbor according to the flesh. When the pressures and trials come (and they will) to test your heart, stand on the Word of God and love your neighbor. This is how the flesh dies. Resist all temptations to defraud, hate, exploit, or speak against your neighbor. If he has done any wrong, God's vengeance will take care of him. Let God be the judge. When you refuse to speak any words against your neighbor, you are then putting to death the flesh and you are ceasing from sin. When you are reviled, persecuted and insulted, you speak blessings. You put to death the deeds of the flesh by resisting the flesh. You are dying to the ways of Satan and your mind is being renewed, because you are choosing to have the mind of Christ. You prove you love the nature of God more than the nature of the devil. Your heart believes unto righteousness.

"Consider it all joy, my brethren, when you encounter various trials, knowing that the testing of your faith produces endurance. And let endurance have its perfect result, that you may be *perfect* (perfected in love) and *complete* (a mature man with a pure heart), lacking in nothing" (James 1:2-4). "But put on the Lord Jesus Christ, and *make no provision for the flesh in regard to its lusts*" (Rom. 13:14). "Is the law then contrary to the promises of God (our covenant with Jesus)? May it never be! ..." (Gal. 3:21).

On the one hand, the law brings judgment and wrath on all who do not keep the law. On the other hand, Jesus tells us to come to Him and He will lead us to fulfill the law by becoming a doer of the law. This is how we are saved from the destruction and judgment of God's law. "... IF you are led by the Spirit, you are not under (the judgment of) the Law" (Gal. 5:18).

Put To Death The Flesh To Have A Pure Heart

The powers of darkness come to entice and tempt the brethren to break the law so that they can devour us. "Be of sober spirit, be on the alert. Your adversary the devil (powers of darkness) prowls about like a roaring lion, *seeking someone* (brethren) *to devour* (destroy). But *resist him, firm* in your *faith* (only the brethren have faith), knowing that the same experiences of *suffering* (you suffer in the flesh when you resist anger, unforgiveness, resentment, etc.) *are being accomplished by your brethren* who are in the world. And *after* you have *suffered for a little while* (when you prove that you love God more than you love the flesh by purifying your heart), the God of all grace, who called you to His eternal glory in Christ, *will Himself perfect (you), confirm (you), strengthen (you) and establish you* (in your covenant walk with Jesus)" (I Pet. 5:8-10).

We suffer as we deny ourselves and resist the fleshly temptations of Satan. We will suffer for a little while, putting to death the fleshly desires, because we love Jesus more than we love the flesh. This was the commandment of the law that we first love the Lord with all our hearts.

The Lord then leads us to die to the selfish flesh in order to have the nature of God and love our neighbor as ourselves: "For you are all *sons of God* through faith in Christ Jesus" (Gal. 3:26). The real sons of God put to death the flesh in order to have a pure heart.

The result of this faith is to become *doers* of the law by loving their neighbor as themselves. "Do we then nullify the law through faith? May it never be! On the contrary, we establish (fulfill) the law" (Rom. 3:31).

We fulfill the law by being led by the Spirit of God (faith) to become doers of the law. Jesus Christ came to fulfill the law in us so we could be reconciled to God: "For Christ is the end of the law for righteousness to everyone who believes" (Rom. 10:4). If we believe, we will be perfected in love to fulfill the law.

Paul explains how he was set free through the Lord Jesus Christ: "So then, brethren, we are *under obligation*, not to ... live according to the flesh (breaking God's law) — for if you are (still) living according to the flesh, *you must die;* but if (you are living) by the Spirit (faith) *you are putting to death the deeds of the body* (the lawless flesh nature), you will *live*. For ALL who are being *led by the Spirit of God, these are the SONS OF* God" (Rom. 8:12-14). "If you are led by the Spirit, you are not under the (judgment of the) law (because we fulfill the law through *obedience)*" (Gal. 5:18).

Obedience
Is Not Legalism

When someone suggests to those who follow a form of godliness that we are required to be obedient to the com -

mandments of God, you sometimes hear accusations of "legalism." The majority of the church today is trying to guard against being trapped in the error of legalism as were the Pharisees. The Pharisees were very legalistic by setting up their own rules. Then obedience to their rules became their standard for fulfilling God's law.

When we attempt to fulfill God's law through obeying our own set of rules, this is legalism and the works of the flesh. We are not being led and controlled by the Spirit of God. When the Pharisees became legalistic by obeying their own set of laws and rules, they were blinded to the obedience God requires to His own laws. They fulfilled their own set of rules and laws but became transgressors of God's laws. This produced a false security. Almost all of the church today is legalistic in a very similar way. They have drifted away into a form of godliness and they, like the Pharisees, have established their own righteousness. This is accomplished when we believe our righteousness is fulfilled in the fleshly works of carnal doctrines. This is the "peace and safety" message today.

Carnal doctrines are only partial truths which have fulfilled the selfish ambition of men but do not fulfill the spiritual laws of God. Those who follow carnal doctrines are in spiritual darkness because they are not led by the Spirit of God to fulfill the law of God. They remain under the judgment of the law with a false security. There is no protection from God because of their disobedience. *This is why the powers of darkness are in the church today.*

Legalism captured the hearts of the Pharisees. They had developed a very complex system of do's and don'ts. They were constantly rebuking anyone who dared to disobey the rules they had developed.

When Jesus refused to subject Himself and His disciples to their regulations, they were quick to criticize. They said to Jesus: " 'Why do Your disciples transgress the tradition of the elders?' ... And He answered and said to them, 'And why do you yourselves transgress the commandments of God for the sake of your traditions?' " (Matt. 15:2, 3). This is a form of godliness.

All of their regulations were being observed without once honoring the Lord from their heart. Jesus said to them, "... There is *nothing outside* the man which going into him can defile him; but the things which proceed out of the (mouth of) man are what defile the man (because it comes from his heart). For from within, *out of the heart* of men, proceed ... deeds of coveting and wickedness, as well as deceit, sensuality, envy, slander, pride ... (which break God's commandments). All these *evil things* proceed from *within* (the heart) and *defile the man"* (Mark 7:15, 21-23).

We see a distinction in the efforts of man to please God outwardly by obeying a set of regulations while his heart continues to break God's law with slander, pride and other sins.

While the Pharisees were carrying out the desires of the flesh and looking good outwardly, the Lord was looking into their hearts. The issue to God is, does a man love Him with all his heart? "... For God sees not as man sees, for man looks at the outward appearance, but the Lord looks at the heart" (I Sam. 16:7).

The Pharisees were admired by the people for their diligence and godliness because they faithfully carried out and defended their legalistic traditions. But Jesus said to them, "Woe to you, scribes and Pharisees, hypocrites! For you are like whitewashed tombs which on the outside appear beautiful, but inside they are full of dead men's bones and all uncleanness. Even so you too outwardly appear righteous to men, but *inwardly* you are full of hypocrisy and lawlessness (sin)" (Matt. 23:27, 28).

The legalism of the Pharisees consisted of traditions which could be carried out with outward works of the flesh: "Do not handle, do not taste, do not touch! They were in accordance with the commandments and teachings of men. These are matters which have, to be sure, the appearance of wisdom in self-made religion and self-abasement and severe treatment of the body, but are of *NO VALUE AGAINST FLESHLY INDULGENCE"* (Col. 2:21-23).

The church today is filled with similar kinds of legalistic rules and regulations. Each structure has its own set of rules. But like the Pharisees, they are only works of the flesh, a form of godliness, which can never lead people to truly love their neighbor and fulfill God's law.

The flesh nature constantly looks for rules it can fulfill without having to take up the cross and deal with the heart. Much of the church is caught in that same trap today. The rules of these structures, like the rules of the Pharisees, are of no value against the rebellious nature of the flesh. *OBEDIENCE TO THE COMMANDMENTS OF GOD IS NOT LEGALISM. LEGALISM IS OBEDIENCE TO THE COMMANDMENTS OF MEN.*

This is why James says, "... faith, if it has no works (fruit of obedience) is dead, being by itself" (James 2:17). Works of love are the direct result of obedience and walking in faith.

All the legalistic works of the flesh will never satisfy the Lord's demand for obedience to His law. Even the "sacrifices of praise" being offered up to the Lord in church today are meaningless unless they come from hearts that are obedient to His Word.

The truth Samuel spoke to King Saul still stands true, "... Has the Lord as much delight ... in ... sacrifices as in *obeying* the voice of the Lord? Behold, to obey is better than sacrifice ... for rebellion is as the sin of divination, and insubordination is as iniquity and idolatry" (I Sam. 15:22, 23).

Obedience is the *only way* we can walk in the love that God requires in His law. By this obedience to His Spirit, we "... become conformed to the image of His Son (Jesus)" (Rom. 8:29).

Jesus invites us to come to Him with all our heart so He can lead us to be perfected in His covenant of love. Totally through His grace, He makes us strong enough to become doers of the law. "... He who began a good work in you will perfect it until the day of Christ Jesus" (Phil. 1:6).

However, if you are not ready to give up everything in the world and everything of the flesh, you are not ready to make Jesus Christ Lord. Jesus cannot perfect a good work in you if you walk in disobedience. If you love sin more than you love Jesus, you have a hardened heart. You will not submit to the obedience of the Spirit to be perfected in love.

The Lord Empowers Us To Overcome The Flesh

"For since He Himself was tempted (after the lusts of the flesh) in that which He has suffered, He is able to come to the aid of those who are tempted (after the flesh)" (Heb. 2:18). "For we do not have a high priest who cannot sympathize with our weaknesses (of the flesh), *but one who has been tempted in all things AS WE ARE* , yet without sin ... therefore draw near with confidence to the throne of grace, that we may receive MERCY and *may find GRACE to help (resist the devil) in time of need*" (Heb. 4:15, 16).

Understand that *mercy* and *grace* empower us to resist the temptations of the flesh which come from Satan. Mercy and grace have been perverted by carnal doctrines which tell us we can practice the desires of the flesh (lawlessness) without judgment.

They say, "No one can keep the law." That is true if you follow a form of godliness, but if you follow Jesus you receive mercy and grace to become doers of the law. How can you have the mind of Christ if you continue walking with the mind of the devil? God is commanding us to be conformed to the image of Jesus without reservation.

The sons of God are those who are justified by faith and this faith leads us to fulfill the law. His Spirit leads us to put to death all the deeds of the lawless flesh nature. This must happen so your heart can be purified and love your neighbor as yourself. *You have then laid down your life.* This is the only way we can walk in the love that God demands. "... He has granted to us His precious and magnificent promises, in order that by them (the Word of God) you might become partakers of the *DIVINE NATURE*, having escaped the corruption (judgment of death) that is in the world by *lust* (of the flesh)" (II Pet. 1:4). We then have the nature of God and *we love others as Jesus has loved us.*

"Since you have in obedience to the truth PURI-FIED your souls for a sincere love of the brethren, fervently love one another from the heart, for you have been *born again* ... through the living and abiding Word of God" (I Pet. 1:22, 23).

The Word conforms us to the image of Jesus, holy and blameless. We then have the divine nature of God and bear the fruit of love. The opposite of this is to love the flesh and have our minds set on things of the world and build our treasures here on earth. "For where your treasure is, there will your heart be also" (Matt. 6:21).

"For this you know with certainty, that no immoral or impure person or covetous man, who is an idolater (continues to practice sin), has an inheritance in the kingdom of Christ and God. *LET NO ONE DECEIVE YOU WITH EMPTY WORDS, FOR BECAUSE OF THESE THINGS THE WRATH OF GOD* (judgment of the law) *COMES UPON THE SONS OF DISOBEDIENCE* (who walk after fleshly desires). *Therefore do not be partakers with them;* for you were formerly darkness, but now walk as children of light. For this reason it says, *'AWAKE SLEEPER, and arise from the* (judgment of the) *dead* ... Be careful how you walk ... understand what the will of the Lord is ... *that He might present to Himself the church in all her glory, having no spot or wrinkle or any such thing;* but that she should be *HOLY* and *BLAMELESS* ... that He might *SANCTIFY HER* (purify her heart), *having cleansed her by the washing of the water with the word'* " (Eph. 5:5-8, 14, 15, 17, 27, 26). These scriptures clearly explain that sanctification is being cleansed by the Word of God in order to be holy and blameless.

God is now warning us to *wake up* in order to escape the judgment and wrath of God. "... The law has become our tutor to lead us to Christ, that we may be *justified by faith*" (Gal. 3:24). Remember that we are led to Christ and then justified by faith. We have already seen that "... *not* the hearers of the law are just before God, but the *doers of the law* (who walk in love) will be *JUSTIFIED*" (Rom. 2:13).

How We Become
Slaves Of Righteousness

Being justified by faith means we are justified through Jesus who leads us to become doers of the law, which means walking in love. It is natural to keep the law when our hearts are pure because we then have the nature of God. But those who follow after carnal doctrines oppose this truth because they are lovers of self and trust their form of godliness.

When we come to the Lord we are to love Him with all our heart; more than the world, more than the things in the world, more than family, more than the desires of the flesh, more than anything. Then the Word of God is able to wash our hearts from all unrighteousness because our motives and desires of our hearts are now to please Jesus. We want to please Him more than to fulfill our desires for pride, greed, selfishness, building treasures in this world, or anything else. We no longer present our members (our bodies) as slaves to sin, but as slaves to righteousness.

Paul gave us an example of this walk: "But whatever things were gain to me, those things I have counted as loss for the sake of Christ ... I count all things to be loss in view of the surpassing value of knowing Christ Jesus my Lord, for whom I have suffered the loss of *all things*, and count them but rubbish in order that I may *gain Christ* and may be found in Him, not having a righteousness of my own derived from the Law, but that which is through faith in Christ, the righteousness which comes from God on the basis of faith (obedience), that I may know Him, and the power of His resurrection and the fellowship of His sufferings (by denying flesh), being conformed to His death (Paul took up his cross by denying himself and laying down his life in the flesh) in order that I may attain to the resurrection from the dead (salvation)" (Phil. 3:7-10). Paul has just explained how he was being perfected in love. God has given us the very same instruction to die to sin.

"For you (also) have been called for this purpose, since Christ also suffered for you, leaving you an example for you to follow in His steps" (I Pet. 2:21)."Therefore since Christ has suffered in the flesh, arm yourselves also with the same purpose, because he who has suffered in the flesh has ceased from sin; (breaking God's laws) so as to live ... *no longer* for the *lusts* of men, but for the *will of God* (sanctification, a pure heart)" (I Pet. 4:1, 2). "And if children ... and fellow heirs with Christ, if indeed we suffer with Him in order that we may also be glorified with Him" (Rom. 8:17). "Always carrying about in the body the dying of Jesus, that the life of Jesus also may be manifested in our body. For we who live are constantly being delivered over to death for Jesus' sake, *that the life of Jesus* (holy and blameless) *also may be manifested in our mortal flesh*" (II Cor. 4:10, 11). "For if we have become united with Him in the likeness of His death, certainly we shall be also in the likeness of His resurrection" (Rom. 6:5). God did not have one gospel for Paul and another gospel for us. Both Jesus and Paul were living examples for us today.

A good question would be: "Did the first church in Acts, which is our true example for the church today, really forsake all to love their neighbors as themselves?" "All those who had believed were *together*, and *had all things in common;* and they began selling their property and possessions, and were sharing them with all, as anyone might have need. And day by day continuing with *one mind* in the temple ... the *congregation* of those who believed were of one heart and soul; and not one of them claimed that anything belonging to him was his own; but all things were *common property to them* ... and abundant grace was upon them all. For there was not a needy person among them ..." (Acts 2:44-46; 4:32-34).

I could ask the question again, "Did they love their neighbor as themselves?" "Did they love one another as Christ had loved them?" This church set the example for us by having the nature of God as did Jesus and Paul. What happened to this gospel? Is there another gospel? The answer is *THE LAW HAS BEEN LOST*. There is no fear of God. The church in the days of Acts knew they were to forsake all and be perfected in love.

The rich young ruler came to Jesus to find out what he must do to "... inherit eternal life? And Jesus (referring to the law) said to him ... you know the commandments, 'Do not murder, Do not commit adultery, Do not steal, Do not bear false witness' ... and he said to Him, 'Teacher, I have kept all these things from my youth up.' ... (Jesus) said to him, *'One thing you lack:* go and *sell all you possess*, and give to the poor, and *you shall have treasure in heaven'* ; (I still do not have all of your heart) and (then) COME, FOLLOW ME' " (Mark 10:17-21).

God demands all of our hearts. If He does not have all of our hearts, then we will turn to the treasures of the world. If God has all our hearts, we will then build our treasures in heaven. We remain on this earth for only a short time to pass through the trials of this world and prove to God that we love Him with all our hearts.

Jesus said to the rich young ruler "... If you wish to be *COMPLETE*, go and sell your possessions ..." (Matt. 19:21.) Jesus said these things because He saw that greed still had the heart of the rich young ruler: *"At these words, his face fell and he went away grieved (because he loved greed more than he loved God);* for he was one who owned much property. And Jesus ... said to His disciples, 'How hard it will be for those who are wealthy to enter the kingdom of God!' " (Mark 10:22, 23).

Many who read this verse are amazed and astonished at these words and wonder, "Well, who can be saved?"

The disciples were amazed and astonished about these words as we are: "and the disciples were amazed at His words. But Jesus answered again and said to them, 'Children, how hard it is to enter the kingdom of God!' And they were even *more astonished* and said to Him, *'Then who can be saved?'* Looking upon them, Jesus said, 'With men it is impossible ... ' Peter began to say to Him, 'Behold, we have left everything and followed You.' Jesus said, 'Truly I say to you, there is no one who has left house or brothers or sisters or mother or father or children or farms, for My sake, and for the gospel's sake, but that he shall receive a hundred times as *much now in the present age ... along with persecutions; and in the age to come, ETERNAL LIFE ...* And they were amazed and those who followed were *fearful* ..." (Mark 10:24, 26-30, 32).

If the disciples were amazed, astonished and fearful at these statements of Jesus, why shouldn't we be even more astonished today? However, these same disciples later taught these things to the first church of the Lord Jesus Christ. This church sold all its property and shared with all who had need. They were building their treasures in heaven. All things were common property. They loved their neighbors more than they loved greed. This church was perfected in the unity of the faith and the fulness of the same stature which belonged to Christ. They were of one heart and one mind in the temple because Jesus was the center, not man.

No one can receive these scriptures unless Jesus has all of his heart. Did Jesus tell us to lay down our lives in this world? If we lay down our life for our neighbor, then what do we own in this world? The implications of these scriptures will cause a cultural shock to those in the worldly church today. We have been led astray. We find all kinds of patterns in this world that are called the church that we are to become like. But the disciples who spent years with the Lord knew exactly what the church was supposed to be like. They left us this example in the book of Acts.

When we love the Lord with all our hearts, it costs us everything in this life and in this world. The Spirit of God can then totally control our lives and Satan can do nothing because all selfishness is removed. This church puts into practice the commandments of our Lord to love their neighbors as themselves, and to love one another as Jesus had loved them.

If we look at these scriptures through the eyes of a form of godliness, we will call this a history of the church, rather than a revelation of the church of Jesus Christ which was to be perfected in love.

Not only was the rich young ruler required to sell all that he had to follow Jesus, but many in the first church in the book of Acts felt led to do the same. The powers of darkness could no longer tempt their hearts with one thing in this world. They built all their treasures in heaven, because they had laid down their lives for their neighbors. They laid down their lives to please God and be vessels to extend God's love to the whole world, because they now had the nature of Jesus.

Listen to the Word: "For we also once were foolish ourselves, disobedient, deceived, enslaved to various lusts and pleasures, spending our lives in malice and envy, hateful, hating one another. (But) He saved us ... by the washing of regeneration (cleansing our hearts with the Word of God) and renewing (of the mind) by the Holy Spirit (to have the mind of Christ)" (Titus 3:3, 5). This is sanctification. This is how we are conformed to the image of Jesus and become the blameless bride of Christ.

We now walk and talk like our Lord and no longer according to the flesh. We can clearly see what grace and salvation instruct us to do in Titus 2:11-14: "For the *grace* of God has appeared, bringing *salvation* to all men, *instructing us to deny ungodliness and worldly desires* and to live sensibly, righteously and godly in the present age, looking for the blessed hope ... who gave Himself for us, that HE MIGHT REDEEM US FROM *EVERY LAWLESS DEED* and *PURIFY* for Himself a people for His own possession, (holy and) zealous for good deeds (to walk in love)."

Jesus commanded the body of Christ to lay down their lives in order that we may love our friends as He has loved us. Paul identified this body of Christ by saying, "Now those who belong to Christ Jesus have crucified the flesh with its passions and desires" (Gal. 5:24). "But all things become visible when they are exposed by the light" (Eph. 5:13).

We Are Called
To Holiness

Jesus is calling you to holiness: "... Work out your salvation with fear and trembling; for it is God who is at work in you ... that you may prove yourselves to be blameless and innocent, children of God above reproach in the midst of a crooked and perverse generation, among whom you appear as lights in the world" Phil. 2:12, 13, 15.

When we are led by the Spirit of God, we no longer walk after the flesh. We bear a different fruit, the fruit of love, the nature of God: "... AGAINST SUCH THINGS THERE IS NO LAW" (Gal. 5:23). This is how Christ fulfills the law in us. His Spirit leads us to be doers of the law, because we have a new heart, a pure heart and new fruit, the fruit of love. We no longer break the law, but *we fulfill the law.*

We are now walking in God's protection and blessings because we love God with all our hearts and our neighbors as ourselves. We have ceased from our works and have entered into the rest of God: "For the law of the spirit of life in Christ Jesus has set you free from the law of sin and death, in order that the *REQUIREMENTS OF THE LAW* might be *FULFILLED IN US* WHO ..." DO WHAT?

1. Join a religious structure?
2. Find the best doctrine?
3. Manifest a spiritual gift?
4. Do works for Jesus?
5. Etc., etc., etc.

No! No! No! No! No! No! No! No!

"*... That the requirement of the law might be fulfilled in us, WHO DO NOT WALK ACCORDING TO THE FLESH, but according to the Spirit*" (Rom. 8:4). "... WALK BY THE SPIRIT, AND YOU *WILL NOT* CARRY OUT THE DESIRE OF THE FLESH ... IF you are *LED BY THE SPIRIT*, you are *NOT UNDER THE* (judgment of the) *LAW* (because you fulfill the law)" (Gal. 5:16, 18). This is the true church of the Lord Jesus Christ.

The true church is not under the law. They are led by the Spirit of God to put to death the deeds of the flesh so they can be perfected in love and fulfill the law. This is the church which can say, "We are no longer under the judgment and curses of the law." The false church, which follows a form of godliness, is a dwelling place of demons because she transgresses the law instead of fulfilling the law of love.

The Grace Of God Has Been Perverted

The grace of God does not permit us to practice sin as carnal doctrines teach us today: "What then? Shall we sin because we are not under the law but *under grace? MAY IT NEVER BE!* ... Are we to *continue in sin* (practicing sin) that *grace* might increase? *MAY IT NEVER BE!* How shall we who died to sin still live in it? But thanks be to God that though you *were* slaves of sin, you became obedient from the heart to that form of teaching *(THE GOSPEL)* to which you were committed and having been freed from sin, you became slaves of righteousness (love)" (Rom. 6:15, 1, 2, 17, 18).

Our obedience to the Word of God and the Spirit of God perfects in us the God-kind of love and righteous - ness: *"BUT WHOEVER KEEPS HIS WORD, IN HIM THE LOVE OF GOD HAS TRULY BEEN PER- FECTED. BY THIS WE KNOW THAT WE ARE IN HIM (IN CHRIST):* the one who says he abides in Him ought himself to walk in the same manner as He walked" (I John 2:5, 6).

This is the body of Christ, perfected in love. If Jesus commands us to love one another with the same love with which He loved us, *WOULD HE NOT EXPECT US TO DO IT?* This is the very same love which causes you to love your neighbor as yourself.

Many people in congregations today find security in the works they do for God. They sincerely believe if they do works for God that it is all right to practice sin (lawlessness). However, the Word of God teaches just the opposite. We no longer present the members of our body as slaves to impurity and lawlessness (practicing sin): "Many will say to Me on that day, 'Lord, Lord, did we not prophesy in Your name, and in Your name cast out demons, and in Your name perform many miracles?' And then I will declare to them, 'I never knew you; depart from Me, you who *practice lawlessness* (who continued to practice sin)' " (Matt. 7:22, 23). "Everyone who *practices sin* also practices lawlessness; and *sin is lawlessness"* (I John 3:4). This is how the fallen-away church walks today.

We continue to break the law if we continue to practice sin. Paul said, "... If, while seeking to be justified in Christ, we ourselves have also been found sinners, is Christ then a minister of sin?" (Paul was saying, in effect: "Are you really being led by the Spirit of God?") MAY IT

NEVER BE! For if I rebuild (the cursed flesh nature) what I have once destroyed, I prove myself to (still) be a transgressor (and still walking under the judgment of the law)" (Gal. 2:17, 18).

Works Of Flesh Destroyed

Paul said, "You foolish Galatians ... Are you so foolish? Having begun by the Spirit, are you now being perfected (in love) by the flesh?" (Gal. 3:1, 3). This is how people walk under the judgment of the law and under the works of the law, by trying to be perfected in love through the works of the flesh. This brings the curse of the law: "For as many as are of the *works of the law are under a curse* ..." (Gal. 3:10).

We see again the curse of the law is on all those who try to fulfill the law other than being led by the Spirit of God. It is only through being led by the Spirit that we can be perfected in the love that fulfills the law: "So then those who are of faith (led by the Spirit) are *blessed with Abraham* ..." (Gal. 3:9).

This helps explain the blessings and curses of God's law. We will see a clearer explanation as we continue. This is why the hedge is down on a harlot church today. She is trying to be perfected in love after the strength and works of the flesh. This is how Babylon, the harlot church, the church of the last days, becomes a dwelling place of demons (Rev. 18:2): "Little children, *let no one deceive you, the one who practices righteousness is righteous* ... the one who *practices sin* is of the *devil* ... *No one who is born of God practices sin* ... *By this the children of God and the children of the devil are obvious: anyone who does not practice righteousness is not of God, nor the one who does not love his brother*" (I John 3:7-10).

When we continue to practice sin, we are not being controlled by the Spirit of God. We are being controlled by the flesh and sin. We are still choosing to walk in the image of Satan rather than the image of God: "If you know that He is righteous, you know that everyone also who practices righteousness is born of Him" (I John 2:29).

Who Are The False Sons Of God?

"Therefore ... let us also lay aside every encumbrance, and the sin which so easily entangles us, and let us run with endurance the race (to be perfected in love) that is set before us, fixing our eyes on Jesus, the author and *perfecter of faith* ... For consider Him who has endured such hostility by sinners against Himself, so that you may not grow weary and lose heart ... My son, do not regard lightly the discipline of the Lord, nor faint when you are reproved by Him; for those whom the Lord loves He disciplines and He scourges every son whom He receives" (Heb. 12:1-3, 5, 6).

When we repent and come to the Lord with a whole heart, He places a hedge around us so that we walk in peace. Should we find ourselves not walking in peace, the powers of darkness are attacking us. The hedge has been removed because of some sin which has broken God's commandment of love (the law). This is God's discipline and reproof on a Christian who sins. Since we want to repent, we ask the Spirit of God what sin we have committed because we know that we love Jesus more than any sin. The Spirit of God, at some point, will reveal to us the sin. Then, because of the cross, because of the blood of Jesus and His victory over sin, and because He became our sacrifice for sin, the blood of Jesus cleanses us from this sin. We are then forgiven and we are no longer transgressors of God's law. The powers of darkness have no more ground, so they have to back off and the hedge returns. Then we are back in our walk of peace.

As we learn to walk in the blessings and peace of God, we become more and more sensitive about avoiding sin. This is the discipline that leads us to purify our hearts and love others as Jesus has loved us: "It is for discipline that you endure ... But *IF YOU ARE WITHOUT DISCIPLINE (to be perfected in love), OF WHICH ALL (THE BODY OF CHRIST) HAVE BECOME PARTAKERS, THEN YOU ARE ILLEGITIMATE CHILDREN AND NOT SONS (false sons)*" (Heb. 12:7, 8).

False sons refuse to give up their love for the flesh nature of Satan. They devise ways to enter heaven without denying their flesh. They justify themselves with their form of godliness because they still love the world and the flesh. They are not led by the Spirit of God. This is the fallen-away church today.

False sons do not know about the peace of God or the fear of God. Since they walk in a false security, they do not have to sanctify or purify their hearts. Therefore, as they continually break God's law, the powers of darkness are able to lay chain on top of chain, until they are destroyed because they did not choose the nature of God: "There were those who dwelt in darkness and the shadow of death, prisoners in misery and chains, because they had rebelled against the words of God, and spurned the counsel of the Most High. Fools, because of their rebellious way, and because of their iniquities, were afflicted" (Ps. 107:10, 11, 17).

"Furthermore, we had earthly fathers to discipline us ... shall we not much rather be subject to the Father of spirits, and *live?* For they disciplined us for a short time as seemed best to them, but He disciplines us (to put to death the flesh nature) for our good, that we may SHARE HIS HOLINESS (a pure heart)" (Heb. 12:9, 10).

We are obedient children led by the Spirit of God to be perfected in love and holiness: *"AS OBEDIENT CHILD-*

REN, do not be conformed to the former lusts (of the flesh) which were yours in your ignorance (darkness), but *like the Holy One* (Jesus) who called you, *BE HOLY YOUR-SELVES IN ALL YOUR BEHAVIOR* (fulfilling God's law), because it is written, *'You shall be holy, for I am holy.'* And if you address as Father the One *who impartially judges* (with the Law) *according to each man's work, CON-DUCT YOURSELVES IN FEAR DURING THE TIME OF YOUR STAY UPON THE EARTH* (that you may not be destroyed)" (I Pet. 1:14-17).

It is a painful thing to die to the flesh. We have to totally depend upon God. We become broken vessels. It does not look like victory to the world and to those who love a form of godliness: *"All discipline for the moment seems not to be joyful*, but sorrowful: yet to those who have been *trained by it*, afterwards it yields the *PEACEFUL FRUIT OF RIGHTEOUSNESS"* (Heb. 12:11).

Discipline causes us to yield the peaceful fruit of "... love, joy, peace, patience, kindness, goodness, faithfulness, gentleness, self-control; *against such things there is no judgment of the law"* (Gal. 5:22, 23). This is the body of Christ which fulfills the law by submitting to discipline in obedience to the Spirit of God. This is the only way we can have a pure heart. This is sanctification and the walk of peace. *"Pursue PEACE with all men, and the SANCTI-FICATION WITHOUT WHICH NO ONE WILL SEE THE LORD"* (Heb. 12:14).

Paul encouraged the Thessalonians about the opposition and trials which were coming upon the churches of the Lord Jesus Christ. This is the fire which we go through to become vessels of gold and honor.

Paul said, "For you, brethren, became imitators of the churches of God in Christ Jesus ... for you also endured the same sufferings at the hands of your own countrymen, even as I did ..." (I Thess. 2:14). "And we sent Timothy ... to *strengthen* and *encourage* you as to your *faith*, so that no man may be disturbed by these afflictions; for you yourselves know that we have been destined for this ... we kept telling you in advance that we were going to suffer afflictions; and so it came to pass, as you know. For this reason, when I could endure it no longer, I also sent to find out about your *FAITH*, for fear that the *TEMPTER* might have *TEMPTED YOU*, and (you fall away from the faith so that) *our labor should be in vain"* (I Thess. 3:2-5).

Paul was fearful that they would not stand in the trials and persecutions to be perfected in love. He feared that through the temptations, trials and pressures of the powers of darkness, they would turn from the faith back to the ways of the flesh. Therefore they could not be perfected in love to become complete, holy and blameless.

An example of this is in the parable of the word: "Now the parable is this: the seed is the word of God. And those beside the road (the highway of holiness) are those who have heard; then the devil comes and *takes away the word from their heart, so that they may not believe and be saved.* And those on the rocky soil (hardened hearts) are those who, when they hear, receive the word with joy; and these have no firm root (in Jesus); *THEY BELIEVE FOR A WHILE*, but in time of *TEMPTATION* (by the powers of darkness) *FALL AWAY* (from being perfected in love)" (Luke 8:11-13).

They fall away from being perfected in love when the tempter can cause their hearts to turn from God to love other things more than God. This is how we fall away from the faith.

We next see another heart which fails to be perfected in love in the following verse: "And the seed which fell among the thorns, these are the ones who have heard (the Word of God), and as they go on *their way* (of the flesh) they are choked with worries and riches and pleasures of this (present) life, and *bring no fruit (of love) to maturity."*

They love the world and the ways of the world more than God. They were not perfected in love to bring their fruit to maturity.

How A Disciple's Heart Is Perfected In Love

In the last verse of this parable we see the disciple's heart which is perfected in love: "And the seed in the good soil (good heart), these are the ones who have heard the word in an honest and good heart, and hold it fast, and bear (the) fruit (of love) with perseverance" (Luke 8:15).

Jesus is coming for a bride who is holy and blameless. This bride will be perfected in love and she will love her neighbor as Jesus has loved us.

Paul continued by saying that he was praying for them night and day that we "... may complete what is lacking in your faith. Now may our God and Father Himself and Jesus our Lord direct our way to you ... and (may you) ... *abound in love for one another, and for all men ... so that He may establish your hearts unblamable in holiness ... at the coming of our Lord ...*" (I Thess. 3:10-13).

Paul continued, *"FOR THIS IS THE WILL OF GOD, YOUR SANCTIFICATION* (a pure heart) ... that each of you may know how to possess his *own vessel* in *sanctification* and honor, *not in lustful passion* (of the flesh) ... and that *NO MAN TRANSGRESS AND DEFRAUD HIS BROTHER* ... because the *Lord is the avenger* in all these things, just as we also told you before and *SOLEMNLY WARNED YOU.* For God has not called us for the purpose of impurity (an impure heart), but in SANCTIFICATION (a pure heart). Consequently, *he who rejects this is not rejecting man but the God who gives His Holy Spirit to you*" (I Thess. 4:3-8).

We miss the will of God when we are not sanctified. Christ is returning for a bride who has been perfected in love, a doer of God's law. In these scriptures we clearly see that the Word cleanses our hearts from all love of the flesh. This will not happen unless we first love the Lord and His Word more than any sins of the flesh.

Paul was warning that the tempter would try to turn them from the faith. Then they would not be unblamable in holiness at the coming of our Lord. Paul said, "But the goal of our instruction (the gospel) is love from a pure heart ..." (I Tim. 1:5). This is the purpose of sanctification, to have love from a pure heart.

The man who purifies his heart possesses his vessel in sanctification and honor by overcoming the selfish flesh. This is the church.

This is the bride Jesus Christ is returning for. If anyone rejects the teaching of sanctification because of carnal doctrines, he is rejecting God who gives the Holy Spirit. The Word of God has clearly described the church that our Lord Jesus is coming for:

"Or do you not know that the unrighteous shall not inherit the kingdom of God? Do not be deceived; neither fornicators, nor idolaters, nor adulterers ... nor thieves, nor the covetous ... shall inherit the kingdom of God. And such WERE some of you; but you *WERE WASHED* (by the word of God) ... you were *SANCTIFIED* (pure heart) ... *you were JUSTIFIED ...*" (I Cor. 6:9-11).

"And although you were formerly alienated and hostile in mind (when you loved your flesh nature), engaged in evil deeds (of the flesh), yet He has now reconciled you in His fleshly body through death, in order to present you before Him holy and blameless (a pure heart) and beyond reproach —*if indeed you continue in the faith* ... the mystery which has been hidden ... but has now been manifested (through His Son) ... which is Christ (formed) in you, the hope of glory. And we proclaim Him ... that we may present every man complete (with a pure heart, sanctified) in Christ" (Col. 1:21-23, 26-28).

4

The Falling Away and the Fiery Trials

God warns the church today, " 'Do not harden your hearts (by loving other things more than God) as when they provoked Me, as in the day of trial in the wilderness … Therefore I was angry with this generation; they always *go astray in their hearts;* and they did not know My ways; as I swore in My wrath, they shall not enter My rest, (peace).'

"Take care, brethren, lest there should be in any one of you an evil, unbelieving heart, in falling away from the living God … lest any one of you be *hardened* by the deceitfulness of sin (return to sin).

"For we have become partakers of Christ, IF we hold fast the beginning of our assurance firm until the end (overcome)" (Heb. 3:8, 10-14).

The simple explanation of falling away would be the fact that the Bible states that you can fall away from the faith.

A person falls away from the faith when his heart turns to love other things more than God.

This is idolatry.

When his heart turns from God, he is unable to enter into rest and peace because he turns back to sin and once again breaks God's laws.

Israel, An Example
For Us Today

Like the children of Israel, we are commanded to possess the land by overcoming sin. This is the way we enter into the land of rest and peace. Our hearts are tested as their hearts were tested. When we walk in obedience to the Spirit of God, we are protected and receive the blessings of God. When we walk in disobedience by choosing the ways of the flesh, the law brings the curse and death if we continue to practice sin: "... If you are living according to the flesh, you must die ..." (Rom. 8:13).

Because the hedge is down, the powers of darkness can bring adversity and death: "For the mind set on the flesh is death, but the mind set on the Spirit is *life* and *peace* (rest)" (Rom. 8:6).

We cannot enter into the land of rest and peace unless we love the Lord with *all our hearts*. When the Lord has all of our hearts, we are living totally for Him. This is what God demands and this walk eliminates all idolatry. This is the only walk which will overcome and enter into the land of peace and rest.

We take the weapons of God and overcome sin, the world, and the devil. We become the mature man "... to the (same) measure of the stature which belongs to the fullness of Christ" (Eph. 4:13).

This is the land of rest. God has commanded His craftsmen, the apostles, prophets, evangelists, pastors and teachers to lead the body of Christ through the wilderness to possess this land and enter into this rest.

Today we either walk in life or death, the blessings or the curses. We enter into rest and peace by the obedience of faith or we walk in disobedience, in which case we are destroyed by the powers of darkness because we do not have the protection of God.

When the children of Israel were given the law, they were given the same choice, obedience with blessings of God, or disobedience which brought a curse and destruction. They were an example to teach us about God's judgment on disobedience in these last days. *Since the law has been lost to us, we have lost all understanding of the judgment of God and the fear of God.*

Moses said, "See, I have set before you today *LIFE* and prosperity (blessings), and *DEATH* and adversity (curses); in that I command you today to love the Lord your God, to walk in His ways and to keep His commandments and His statutes and His judgments ... that the Lord your God may bless you in the land (of rest and peace) where you are entering to possess it. *But if your heart turns away* and you will not obey, but are *drawn away (by temptations) and worship other gods and serve them* (when we serve the flesh we serve the powers of darkness), I declare to you today that *you shall surely perish* (be destroyed). You shall not prolong your days in the land where you are crossing the Jordan to enter and possess it" (Deut. 30:15-18).

Moses also said, "I call heaven and earth to witness against you today, that I have set before you life (to walk after the Spirit) and death (to walk after the flesh), the blessing and the curse. So choose life in order that you may live, you and your descendants, by loving the Lord your God, by obeying His voice, and by holding fast to Him; for this is your life and the length of your days (if you obey God) that you may live in the land ..." (Deut. 30:19, 20).

The children of Israel were delivered out of the bondage of Egypt as we are delivered out of the bondage of the world. God was leading them through the wilderness to test their hearts. If they were obedient they would enter into the promised land; the land of peace and rest from their enemies, the land where God protects His obedient children.

The judgments that God brought upon the children of Israel are an example of the judgments that are brought upon us today. As God has delivered us from the slavery of the world, God delivered them from the afflictions of Egypt: "Thou didst see the affliction of our fathers in Egypt, and didst hear their cry by the Red Sea ... So they passed through the midst of the sea on dry ground ... Thou didst come down on Mount Sinai, and didst speak with them from heaven ... and didst lay down for them commandments, statutes, and laws, through Thy servant Moses" (Neh. 9:9, 11, 13, 14).

Nehemiah continued: "Thou didst provide *bread from heaven* (which is the Word of God today) for them for their hunger, Thou didst bring forth water (the Word) from a rock (Jesus) for them for their thirst, and Thou didst tell them to enter in order to *possess the land* ... They became stubborn (hardened hearts) and *would not listen to Thy commandments*. And they refused to listen ... So they became stubborn and *appointed a leader* (to tickle their ears) to return to their slavery in Egypt (the world) ..." (Neh. 9:15-17).

Congregations fall away from the faith when they appoint a leader who leads them back to the sin and bondage of the world. This is the very opposite of peace and rest: "And there you will serve gods, the work of man's hands, wood and stone ..." (Deut. 4:28).

This is what has happened to the fallen-away church today. They have turned their hearts away from the law of God and have appointed leaders to return to the slavery of the world. They are worshipping the works of man's hands of wood and stone. Like Israel, congregations today have appointed kings and leaders to tickle their ears with a form of godliness so they can justify their worldly lifestyles in the churches. God does not have their hearts. The world has their hearts.

Reading about the children of Israel is just like Moses speaking to us today: "Then I commanded you at that time, saying, 'The Lord your God has given you this land to (overcome and) possess it; all you valiant men shall cross over armed (with the weapons of warfare which they will use to remove the Canaanite nations who are types of the powers of darkness) ... until the Lord gives *rest* to your fellow countrymen as to you, and they also *possess the land* which the Lord your God will give them beyond the Jordan ... ' " (Deut. 3:18, 20). "But they, our fathers, acted arrogantly; they became stubborn and would not listen to Thy commandments" (Neh. 9:16).

The Psalmist wrote on this same issue: "They quickly forgot His works; they did not wait for His counsel, but *craved intensely* (after the flesh) in the wilderness (world) ..." (Ps. 106:13, 14). "They did not keep the covenant of God, and *refused to walk in His law* ... a stubborn and rebellious generation, a generation that *did not prepare its heart*, and whose spirit was not faithful to God" (Ps. 78:10, 8). "They made a calf in Horeb, and worshiped a molten image (a form of godliness). Thus they exchanged their glory (for the image of a beast as it is today) ... They forgot their Saviour ... They did not believe in His word, that He would cast them down in the wilderness (remove the hedge)" (Ps. 106:19-21, 24-26).

The Psalmist also said: "He brought forth streams also from the rock (a type of Jesus) ... yet they still continued to sin against him (hardened their hearts), to rebel against the Most High in the desert. And in their heart they put God to the test by asking food according to their desire (after the flesh)" (Ps. 78:16-18). "... They mingled with the nations (of the world), and *learned their practices, and served their idols*, which became a snare to them. They even sacrificed their sons and their daughters to the demons (this is exactly what we do today by teaching our children's hearts to go after success, power, and treasures of the world). Thus they became unclean in their practices, and *played the harlot in their deeds*. Therefore the anger of the Lord was kindled against His people ... Then He gave them into the hand of the nations; and those who hated them ruled over them (as the powers of darkness have invaded a fallen away church today)" (Ps. 106:35-37, 39-41).

The Psalmist also declared: "Therefore the Lord ... was full of wrath, and a fire was kindled against Jacob, and anger also mounted against Israel; because they did not believe in God, and *did not trust in His salvation*. So He brought their days to an end in futility, and their years in sudden terror. *When He killed them*, then they sought for Him, and returned and searched diligently for God; and they remembered that God was their rock (Jesus), and the Most High their Redeemer. But they deceived Him with their mouth, and lied to Him with their tongue. For their heart was not steadfast toward Him, nor were they faithful in His covenant" (Ps. 78:21, 22, 33-37).

Nehemiah, addressing the same subject, said: "But as soon as they had rest, they did evil again before Thee; Therefore Thou didst abandon them (no protection) to the hand of their enemies, so that they ruled over them ... And many times Thou didst rescue them according to Thy com-passion, and admonished them in order to *turn them back to Thy law*. Yet they acted arrogantly and did not *listen to Thy commandments* but sinned against Thine ordinances, by which if a man observes them he shall live. And they turned a stubborn shoulder and stiffened their neck, and would not listen" (Neh. 9:28, 29).

The Psalmist said, "Many times He would deliver them; They, however, were rebellious in their counsel, and so sank down in their iniquity" (Ps. 106:43).

According to Nehemiah, "... Thou art just in all that has come upon us; for Thou has dealt faithfully, but we have acted wickedly. For our (flesh) kings, our (flesh) leaders, our priests, and our fathers have not kept Thy law or paid attention to Thy commandments ... but they, in their own kingdom ... did not serve Thee or turn from their evil deeds. Behold, we are slaves today, and as to the land ... behold, we are slaves on it. And its abundant produce (fruit) is for the kings whom Thou has *set over us* because of our *sins; They also rule over our bodies ... so we are in great distress*" (Neh. 9:33-37).

The Psalmist said: "For they provoked Him with their high places (as they do today), and aroused His jealousy with their graven images. So that He abandoned the dwelling place at Shiloh (as He has abandoned the fallen away church today) ... and gave up His strength to captivity, and His glory into the hand of the adversary ... and was filled with wrath at His inheritance. *Fire (the powers of darkness) devoured His young men; and His (foolish) virgins had NO WEDDING SONGS*" (Ps. 78:58, 60-63). "Oh God, the nations have invaded Thine inheritance; they have defiled Thy holy temple; they have laid Jerusalem (the church) in ruins. They have given the (spiritually) dead bodies of Thy servants for food to the birds of the heavens (powers of darkness), the flesh of Thy godly ones to the beasts of the earth (the powers of darkness)" (Ps. 79:1, 2).

Only the ones who love the Lord with all their hearts and put their faith and trust in Him will survive the judgment of the law today. The others will be lawbreakers and will be kept under the judgment of the law. "... The Lord knows how to rescue the godly from temptation, and to keep the unrighteous under punishment for the day of judgment, and especially those who indulge the flesh in its corrupt desires and despise authority ..." (II Pet. 2:9, 10).

We either resist the flesh and the temptations of Satan, or else we walk after the desires of the flesh in unrighteousness, staying under the punishment and judgment of God's law. This makes it easier to see and understand that we shall be saved, yet so as through fire.

Israel turned away from entering peace and rest as the church today has turned back from following God. They provoked God to jealousy by turning their hearts to other things instead of Him. Their hearts fell away from God as a fallen church today has departed from God and turned to the ways and idols of the world. God is jealous for our hearts also and warned us of His wrath by using the children of Israel as an example.

Moses wrote: "Beware lest you forget the Lord your God by not keeping His commandments ... then your heart becomes proud, and you forget the Lord your God who brought you out of the land of Egypt, out of the house of slavery. He led you through the great and *terrible wilderness* (world), with its *fiery serpents* and *scorpions* (which are types of the powers of darkness) and thirsty ground where there was no water; He brought *water* for you out of the *rock of flint*" (Deut. 8:11, 14, 15).

As they needed water physically to survive in the wilderness, we also need water today. That water is the Word of God. We need the understanding of God's Word to lead us through the terrible wilderness, in order to obtain God's protection from the fiery serpents. Their physical water was brought out of the rock of flint. Our spiritual water also is brought out of a rock (Jesus).

God is warning us in the New Testament today as He warned the children of Israel to take heed lest we be destroyed as the children of Israel were destroyed because of disobedience. They were examples for us today.

Paul said, "And all drank the same spiritual drink, for they were drinking from a spiritual rock which followed them; and the rock was Christ. Nevertheless, with most of them God was not well-pleased; for they were *laid low* (destroyed) in the wilderness. Now these things happened as *EXAMPLES FOR US, that we should not crave evil things*, as they also craved. And do not be *IDOLATERS*, as some of them were ... nor let us *ACT IMMORALLY, as some of them did, and twenty-three thousand fell in one day* (this is an example and warning for us today). Nor let us *TRY THE LORD*, as some of them did, and were *destroyed by the serpents* (this is an example for us today). Nor *GRUMBLE*, as some of them did, and were *destroyed by the destroyer*" (this is also an example and warning for us today) (I Cor. 10:4-10).

Paul warned: "Now these things happened to them as an example, and *they were written for our instruction upon whom the ends of the ages have come. Therefore let him who thinks he stands take heed lest he fall (away and be destroyed).* No temptation has overtaken you but such as is common to man; and God is faithful, who will not allow you to be tempted beyond what you are able, but with the temptation will provide the way of escape also, that you may be able to endure it. *Therefore, my beloved, FLEE FROM IDOLATRY (from practicing sin).* I speak as to wise men (or wise virgins); you judge what I say. You cannot drink the cup of the Lord (love) and the cup of demons (selfishness); you cannot partake of the table (covenant) of the Lord and the table (covenant) of demons. Or do we (also) provoke the Lord to jealousy? ... *Let no one* seek his own good, but that of his neighbor" (I Cor. 10:11-15, 21, 22, 24).

God warns again that we can fall away in our trials and be destroyed as the children of Israel were destroyed in the wilderness: "... Today if you hear His voice, do not harden your hearts as when they provoked Me, as in the day of trial (of their hearts) in the wilderness" (Heb. 3:7, 8).

We are truly learning the reality of the verses in Matthew 7:13 and 14, "Enter by the narrow gate; for the gate is wide, and *the way is broad that leads to destruction*, and many are those who enter by it. For the gate is *small*, and the way is *narrow* that leads to (eternal) life, and *FEW ARE THOSE WHO FIND IT.*"

Even with all these warnings, the children of Israel refused to fear the Lord and obey Him. The heart of God was grieved by their actions: "Oh that they had such a heart in them, that they would fear Me, and keep all My commandments always, that it may be well with them and their sons forever!" (Deut. 5:20).

The writer of Hebrews said: "And with whom was He angry (on whom did He pour out His judgment) for forty years? *Was it not with those who sinned, whose BODIES FELL in the wilderness?* Therefore *LET US FEAR* lest ... any one of you should seem to have come short of it (the rest and peace of God). ... *Therefore be diligent to enter that rest, lest anyone (also) FALL through following the same example of (their) disobedience"* (Heb. 3:17; 4:11).

The writer added: "For we do not have a high priest who cannot sympathize with our weaknesses (of the flesh), but one who has been tempted in all things AS WE ARE, yet without sin. Let us therefore draw near with confidence to the throne of grace, that we may receive *mercy* and may find *grace* to help (resist the temptations of the devil) in time of need" (Heb. 4:1, 15, 16).

Again, Moses wrote: "... The Lord your God has led you in the wilderness these forty years, that He might humble you, testing you, to know what was in your heart, whether you would keep His commandments or not" (Deut. 8:2).

We are going through these same tests today. We overcome the wilderness experiences of this world in order to enter in and possess the land of peace and rest. These tests will prove whether we really love the Lord with all our hearts. If we love anything more than the Lord, we cannot enter into this peace and rest. A proud person will never stand these tests. Only the humble can be led through the wilderness to the land of peace and rest.

The Fiery Trials

Peter said: "Beloved, do not be surprised at the fiery ordeal among you, which comes upon you for your testing, as though some strange thing were happening to you; but to the degree that you *share the sufferings* of Christ, keep on rejoicing ... Therefore, let those also who suffer according to the *WILL OF GOD* entrust their souls to a faithful Creator in doing what is right" (I Pet. 4:12, 13, 19).

The fiery trials today are the efforts of the world, the flesh and the devil to turn our hearts from God. Every man will either come through the fire and be like gold (with a divine nature) or else he will be a vessel of wood, hay, and stubble, which is burned up. When the pressures and trials come, if we strike back at our neighbor, we break God's law and give the fiery serpents ground to build strongholds and destroy us.

If anyone has a foundation built upon carnal doctrines, they have a false security. The fire will destroy all of those who walk after a form of godliness because they walk in disobedience. Therefore, anyone who stands on this carnal foundation is not standing on the Word of God and their foundation is sand. They are the wood, hay, and stubble in the fiery tests and the fire will consume them because they are not protected by the hedge of God. No other foundation except the Lord Jesus Christ can survive this fire. "... The one who has heard (the Word of God) and *has not acted accordingly*, is like a man who built his house upon the ground *without any foundation;* and the torrent burst against it and immediately it collapsed, and the ruin of that house was great" (Luke 6:49).

Everyone who follows after a doctrine that does not conform them to godliness is destroyed. When you have a false security, you do not act on the Word of God.

Paul wrote: "Now if any man builds upon the foundation with gold, silver and precious stones, wood, hay, straw, each man's work will become evident; for the day (of the Lord) will show it, because it is to be revealed with fire; and the fire (powers of darkness) itself will test the quality of each man's work. For no man can lay a foundation other than the one which is laid, which is Jesus Christ" (I Cor. 3:12, 13, 11).

This is why we need the true apostles, prophets, evangelists, pastors and teachers: "... for the equipping of the saints for the work of service, to the building up of the body of Christ; until *we all attain to the unity of the faith* ... to a *mature man* (pure heart), *to the (same) measure of the stature which belongs to the fulness of Christ* (perfected in love so that we love others as Christ has loved us). As a result, we are no longer to be children, *carried about by every wind of doctrine* (that does not conform us to godliness) ..." (Eph. 4:12-14).

God has been testing the hearts of men since the day He put Adam in the garden. He offered Adam the tree of life or the tree of death. God still tests the hearts of all creation. Only the ones who love the Lord with all their hearts and put their faith and trust in Him will survive the fiery tests of this world. All others will break God's laws and be under the punishment and judgment of the law because their hearts love idols more than God. "... The Lord knows how to rescue the godly from temptation, and to keep the unrighteous under punishment for the day of judgment, and especially those who indulge the flesh in its corrupt desires and despise authority ..." (II Pet. 2:9, 10).

We either resist the flesh and the temptations of Satan, or else we walk after the desires of the flesh in unrighteousness, in which case we stay under the judgment and punishment of God's law.

Jesus said, "... I know your deeds, that you have a name that you are alive, *but you are dead. WAKE UP*, and strengthen the things that remain, which were about to die; for I have not found your *deeds completed* (because you are not being perfected in love) in the sight of my God. Remember therefore what you have received and heard and keep it, and REPENT. If therefore *you will not wake up, I will come like a thief* (in judgment) and you will not know at what hour *I will come upon you.* He who overcomes (the world, flesh and temptations of Satan) shall thus be clothed in white garments; and I will not erase his name from the book of life ..." (Rev. 3:1:3, 5).

Jesus is coming first like a thief in destruction. Jesus did not come the way the religious leaders expected Him the first time. Neither will Jesus come the way the religious leaders expect Him this time. "Hear, you deaf! And look, you blind, that you may see. Who is blind but My servant, or so deaf as My messenger whom I send? ... The Lord was pleased for His righteousness' sake to make the LAW great and glorious. But this is a people plundered and despoiled (lawbreakers) ... hidden away in prisons; they have become a prey (of the powers of darkness) with none to deliver them ... Who among you will give ear to this? Who will give heed and listen hereafter? Who gave Jacob up for spoil, and Israel to plunderers? Was it not the Lord, against whom we have *sinned*, and in *whose ways they were not willing to walk and whose LAW they did not obey?* So He poured out on him the heat of His anger and fierceness of battle (when the hedge is down and the powers of darkness bring death and destruction); and it (the fire) set him aflame all around, *yet he did not recognize it; and it burned him, but he paid no attention"* (Isa. 42:18, 19, 21-25).

The sleeping church is being destroyed today and they don't even know it. They will scoff at warnings such as this. The fire of destruction is already being poured out among us. The scriptures are not enough to lead most of these people out of darkness. This is the reason why there is only a remnant that can hear. The others will not wake up — for them it is business as usual.

God warns us in his Word: " 'It was the same as happened in the days of Lot: they were eating, they were drinking, they were buying, they were selling, they were planting, they were building; but on the day that Lot went out from Sodom it rained fire and brimstone from heaven and *destroyed them all. It will be just the same on the day that the Son of Man is revealed today.* Whoever seeks to keep his (fleshly) life shall lose it, but whoever loses (or lays down) his (fleshly) life shall preserve it. I tell you, on that night (of great spiritual darkness) there will be two men in one bed; one will be *taken* (by the fire) and the other one will be left. Two men will be in the field; one will be *taken* (by the fire) and the other will be left.' And answering they said to Him, *'WHERE, LORD?'* And He said to them, 'Where the (dead) body is, there also will the vultures (the birds of heaven which are the powers of darkness) be gathered' " (Luke 17:28-30, 33, 34, 36, 37).

This is how Jesus comes like a thief upon the spiritually dead congregation that will not wake up and repent in these last days. The hedge is lowered and He no longer restrains the hordes of the powers of darkness which have been unleashed against the spiritually dead, fallen-away church.

If you read these scriptures through the eyes of a carnal doctrine, you will be made to believe that the men who are taken from the bed or out of the field are raptured, rather than destroyed by the fire. This is how deception and darkness have come on us today. This is why people are being burned and they pay no attention. This is the fallen-away church today which practices sin (lawlessness).

The remnant will love the Lord with all their hearts. They will be perfected in love and holiness. No one will be able to counterfeit the love perfected in the remnant. You will know them by their fruits. The stumbling blocks will be evident and they will be destroyed: "He presented another parable to them, saying, 'The kingdom of heaven may be compared to a man who sowed good seed in his field. But while men were *sleeping*, his enemy came and *sowed tares* also among the wheat, and went away. But when the wheat sprang up and *bore grain* (the fruit of love), *then the tares became evident* also (because tares bear the fruit of the flesh)" (Matt. 13:24-26).

"Now the deeds of the flesh are evident ..." (Gal. 5:19). When we practice the deeds of the flesh we bear the wrong fruit and break God's law. This is how men who teach doctrines that do not conform you to godliness lead you to walk under the judgment and curse of the law. This is how the church is being destroyed in the fire today. They have no fear of God as they teach a form of godliness and become stumbling blocks to others. The blind follow the blind and never bear the fruit of love because they are tares: "Therefore just as the tares are gathered up and burned with fire, so shall it be at the end of the age. The Son of Man will send forth His angels, and they will gather out of His kingdom all stumbling blocks, and those who commit lawlessness (by practicing sin)" (Matt. 13:40, 41).

"So it will be at the end of the age; the angels shall come forth, and *take out* the wicked (tares and stumbling blocks) from among the righteous, and will cast them into the furnace of fire (which is the torment and destruction by the powers of darkness); there shall be weeping and gnashing of teeth (hate, anger, bitterness, sickness, pain, unforgiveness, etc.). Then THE RIGHTEOUS WILL SHINE FORTH AS THE SUN in the kingdom of their Father. He who has (spiritual) ears, let him hear" (Matt. 13:49, 50, 43).

There are hundreds of different denominations and teachings in this country today and each one has its own righteousness. But there is only one true righteousness and that is walking right in the eyes of God. When we establish our own righteousness, we do not submit to the righteousness of God. Israel departed from the law and righteousness of God to establish their own righteousness.

Paul said of them "... my prayer to God for them is for their salvation. For I bear them witness that they have a zeal for God, but not in accordance with knowledge (of the Word). For not knowing about God's righteousness, and seeking to establish their own (righteousness) they did not subject themselves to the righteousness of God," (Rom. 10:1-3).

When the wicked thinks he is righteous in his own eyes, he has no fear of God. He is blinded to the judgment of God because of his false security. This is how millions are blinded to the judgment of the law today.

"Listen to Me, you who know righteousness, a people in whose heart is My law; do not fear the reproach of man, neither be dismayed at their revilings. For the *moth* (powers of darkness) will eat them like a garment (because the hedge is removed), and the grub will eat them like wool. But My righteousness shall be forever ..." (Isa. 51:7, 8).

The righteousness of God stands forever because only the righteous will survive. God has set up laws to destroy those who are wise in their own eyes and will not submit to the righteousness of God.

Jesus said: "I am the vine, you are the branches; he who abides (continues) in Me (led by the Spirit) ... he bears much fruit (of love) ... If anyone does not abide (or continue) in Me (falls away) he is thrown away as a branch, and dries up; and *they (the powers of darkness) gather them, and cast them into the (furnace of) fire, and they are burned.* By this is My Father glorified, that you bear much fruit (of love), and so *prove* to be My disciples" (John 15:5, 6, 8).

Jesus sets us free from being slaves of sin (lawlessness) to become slaves of righteousness (a pure heart): "... For just as you presented your members as slaves to impurity and to lawlessness (by practicing the sins of the flesh), resulting in further lawlessness, so now present your mem - bers as slaves to righteousness, resulting in sanctification (a pure heart)" (Rom. 6:19).

Paul said, "Therefore what benefit were you then deriving from the things (sins of the flesh) of which you are now ashamed? For the outcome of those things is *death* (under the judgment and wrath of the law). But now having been *freed from sin* and enslaved to God, you derive your (new) benefit, resulting in sanctification (a pure heart), and *the outcome, ETERNAL LIFE"* (Rom. 6:21, 22).

Through obedience we have a pure heart and we are then perfected in love to the fullness of the measure of the stature which belongs to Christ. When the Word of God has removed the selfish nature of Satan, we no longer live for ourselves. Therefore, we have the nature of God and love others as Jesus loved us. We have laid down our lives so we can walk in God's kind of love. (God's kind of) love is patient, (God's kind of) love is kind, and (God's kind of love) is not jealous; (God's kind of) love ... is not arrogant, does not act unbecomingly, it does not seek its own (selfishness), is not provoked ... (God's kind of love) bears all things, believes all things, hopes all things, endures all things. (God's kind of) love never fails ... If I speak with the tongues of men and of angels, but do not have (this God-kind of) love, I have become a noisy gong or clanging cymbal. And if I have the gift of prophesy, and know all mysteries and have all knowledge; and if I have all faith, so as to remove mountains, but do not have (this God-kind of) love, *I am nothing*. And if I give all my possessions to feed the poor, and if I deliver my body to be burned, but do not have (this God-kind of) love, *it profits me nothing*" (I Cor. 13:4, 5, 7, 8, 1-3).

This God-kind of love is the only love which can love your neighbor as yourself: "For the whole law is fulfilled in one word, in the statement, 'You shall love your neighbor as yourself' " (Gal. 5:14). The ones who come through the fire will have this *GOD-KIND OF LOVE WHICH IS THE DIVINE NATURE OF GOD*.

The Trumpet Is Sounding a Warning to the Fallen-Away Church

Jesus is sounding a warning today for those who have fallen away from the faith: to those who have found a false security in carnal doctrines, and to those who have built their own tower into heaven upon foundations of sand.

Jesus says, "I know your deeds ... because you say, 'I am rich and have become wealthy, and have need of nothing, ' and you *do not know* that you are wretched and miserable and poor and *BLIND* (with no understanding) and *NAKED* (lost by not having the garments of salvation)" (Rev. 3:15, 17).

The warning continues: "I advise you to buy from Me gold (a divine nature) refined by fire (by overcoming the fiery tests), that you may become rich (in God and good works), and white garments (robes of righteousness), that you may clothe yourself, and that the shame of your nakedness (and lostness) may not be revealed; and eyesalve to anoint your eyes, that you may see (and have understanding) ... (because) *THOSE WHOM I LOVE I*

REPROVE AND DISCIPLINE; be zealous therefore, and REPENT (so that you can be perfected in love and holiness) (Rev. 3:18, 19).

Then, He extends an invitation: "Behold, *I stand at the door (of the churches) and knock* (with the Spirit of God); if anyone hears My voice (Word) and opens the door, I will come in to him, and dine (fellowship) with him, and he with Me. He who *overcomes* (the ways of the world, and the unloving works of the flesh and the tests and temptations of the devil), I will grant to him to sit down with Me on My throne, as I also overcame (the world, flesh and devil) and sat down with My Father on His throne. He who has an ear (that can hear), let him hear what the Spirit says to the churches (TODAY)" (Rev. 3:20-23).

Jesus is speaking to the people in fallen-away churches who are without discipline and reproof. Their deeds are not deeds of love because they have refused the discipline needed to be perfected in love. They are illegitimate children.

Jesus warns that the ones He loves are the ones who receive discipline and overcome. These are the ones who will be saved and sit with Him on the throne of His Father. He is telling those who have ears to hear that *they must be sanctified and holy:*

"And it will come about that he who is left in Zion and remains in Jerusalem (the church) will be called holy — everyone who is recorded for life in (the heavenly) Jerusalem. When the Lord has *washed away* the filth (and deeds of the flesh) of the daughters of Zion, and purged the bloodshed of Jerusalem from their midst, by the spirit of judgment (brought by God's law) and the spirit of burning (the fiery trials)" (Isa. 4:3, 4).

"If any man's work (of wood, hay, and stubble which are the works of the flesh and treasures of this world) is burned up, he shall suffer loss (of all these things on earth); but he himself shall be saved (from the ways of the world, the flesh, and the destruction of the powers of darkness), yet so as *through fire* (as he becomes gold, by having the holy nature of God) ... for the temple of God is holy, and that is what you are" (I Cor. 3:15, 17).

The Sin Unto Death

Carnal doctrines and false teachers are leading congregations into a form of godliness. A form of godliness gives congregations a false security and leads them to destruction. They will not receive the discipline and reproof necessary to purify and sanctify their hearts. Their hearts become hardened and the Word can have no place in them.

We are warned that, "False prophets ... and false teachers ... will secretly introduce (not easily discerned) destructive heresies (form of godliness) ... And many will follow their sensuality (flesh), and because of them *the way of truth will be maligned* (perverted); and in their (love for) greed they will exploit you with false words (carnal traditions); their judgment from long ago is not idle, and *their destruction is not asleep* (God's judgment is on them now). For speaking out arrogant words of vanity *they entice (congregations) by fleshly desires* ... promising them freedom (no judgment or curse will come on you) while they themselves are slaves of corruption (flesh nature) ..." (II Pet. 2:1-3, 18, 19).

These false teachers will lead people to turn away from the Word of God through fleshly desires and turn back to the ways of the world: "For if after they have escaped the defilements of the world by the knowledge of the Lord and Saviour Jesus Christ, they are again entangled in them and are overcome, the last state has become worse for them than the first" (II Pet. 2:20).

False teachers will lead congregations from the Word of God through fleshly desires back to loving the ways of the world. As they receive a false security and their hearts return to loving the things of the world, their hearts then become hardened to the Word of God. When this happens, the Word cannot sanctify and purify their hearts because they are not led by the Spirit of God. This is how a church falls away from the faith.

The book of Peter says: "For it would be better for them not to have known the way of righteousness, than having known it, to turn away (fall away) from the holy commandment delivered to them" (II Pet. 2:21).

Since they once knew the way of righteousness and have now turned away from their first love, they will die in their sins because they have been overcome and captured again by the ways of the world: *"For if we go on sinning willfully after receiving the knowledge of the truth, there no longer remains a sacrifice for sins"* (Heb. 10:26). They die in their sins and rebellion.

Since they have put their trust in false teachers and a false security, the Spirit of God cannot lead them out of darkness. If they had not first known the way of righteousness and then hardened their hearts to God's Word, there would *still be an opportunity* for them to yet learn God's righteousness. But now having learned God's righteousness and having hardened their hearts to the holy commandment, their hearts have now become too hardened to return to God's Word. They no longer have a repentant heart. They cannot be perfected in love. They have fallen away from the faith. *THIS IS THE SIN UNTO DEATH!*

"For in the case of those who have once been enlightened and have tasted of the heavenly gift and have been made partakers of the Holy Spirit, and have tasted the good Word of God and of the powers of the age to come, and then have *FALLEN AWAY* (turned back) it is impossible to renew them again to repentance (because they choose to love the very things which God has commanded them to turn from) ..." (Heb. 6:4-6).

Those who have fallen away are those who have become so hardened to the Word of God they will no longer receive the Word into their hearts. They now love other things more than they love God. This is idolatry.

Listen carefully to the Word: "For if we go on sinning willfully after receiving the knowledge of the truth, there no longer remains a sacrifice for sins. (Jesus Christ is the sacrifice for our sins. If we choose to sin willfully, then we are loving other things [idols] in defiance to God. If we do not turn back, we die in our sins because we have no protection from God), but *a certain terrifying expectation of judgment*, and the *fury of a fire* which will consume the adversaries (as it did the children of Israel). For we know Him who said, 'Vengeance is Mine, I will repay'. And again, 'The Lord will judge His people'. It is a terrifying thing to fall into the hands of the living God. But My righteous one shall live by faith (persevere, endure, and overcome); and if he shrinks back, My soul has no pleasure in him" (Heb. 10:26, 27, 30, 31, 38).

Only the ones who love the Lord with all their hearts will not shrink back.

They will receive the mercy and blessings of God. God waits patiently for all others who have these idols to repent and turn to God. If they do not turn, they are destroyed in God's wrath.

Paul said: "What if God, although willing to *demonstrate His wrath* and to make His power known, endured with much patience *vessels (children) of wrath, prepared for destruction?* And He did so in order that He might make known the riches of His glory upon *vessels of mercy* which He prepared beforehand for *glory*" (Rom. 9:22, 23).

God endures with much patience as He waits for us to come to the light and be perfected in love. If our hearts are turned toward other things which we love more than God, we will resist His Word and His Spirit and break His laws.

Therefore, His wrath permits the powers of darkness to continue placing more and more bondage in our lives until we are destroyed. The opposite of this is the vessel of mercy who does not shrink back from the Word of God but walks in faith as he perseveres, endures, and overcomes to be perfected in love.

Everyone who shrinks back from the Word of God does so because his heart has turned from God to love other things more than he loves Christ. This, of course, is the falling away. If he does not repent and turn back, he will be destroyed: "For you have need of endurance, so that when you have done the *will of God*, you may receive what *was promised*. But we are not of those who *SHRINK BACK TO DESTRUCTION*, but of those who *have faith* to the preserving of the soul" (Heb. 10:36, 39).

The Fear
Of The Lord

One of the primary reasons the church today has fallen away from the faith is because it has not learned the fear of God. When God's judgment is not taught, there is no fear of God. We certainly are to reverence God but we are to fear Him also: "My flesh trembles for fear of Thee, and I am afraid of Thy judgments" (Ps. 119:120).

We are taught by carnal doctrines that we can practice sin and there is no reason to fear God. We cannot learn the fear of God until we know truth. When God spoke the commandments of the law from Mount Sinai, the people stood at a distance and trembled. Moses explained, "... God has come in order to test you, and in order *that the fear of Him may remain with you, so that you may not (continue to) sin*" (Ex. 20:20).

When false teachers lead congregations to walk in willful sin, they will not teach about the fear of God because *they have not learned the fear of God*.

Messages about the love of God, unless they are equally balanced with the truth about His judgments upon sin and rebellion, are the "peace and safety" messages of the last days which are leading people to destruction and hell in masses.

God has given us many scriptures about the fear of God: "... And by the fear of God one keeps away from evil" (Prov. 16:6); "The fear of the Lord leads to eternal life" (Prov. 19:23); "The fear of the Lord prolongs life ..." (Prov. 10:27); "The fear of the Lord is the beginning of wisdom ..." (Prov. 9:10); "The fear of the Lord is the beginning of knowledge" (Prov. 1:7); and "My people are destroyed for lack of knowledge" (Hosea 4:6).

Instead of learning the fear of God, we have learned the fear of man.

Man likes to intimidate and be feared so that he can bring people under his fleshly subjection. When you fear man, you can never learn the fear of God. When you fear God, you will never be afraid of man. "The fear of man brings a snare, but he who trusts in the Lord will be exalted" (Prov. 29:25).

Paul wrote: "Now as to the times and the epochs, *brethren*, you have no need of anything to be written to you. For you yourselves know full well that the day of the Lord will come just like a thief in the night (spiritual darkness). While they (the fallen-away church) are saying, 'Peace and safety!' *then destruction* (by the hordes of the powers of darkness) *will come upon them* suddenly like *birth pangs* upon a woman with child; and they shall not escape" (I Thess. 5:1-3).

Then, he adds: *"But you, brethren, are not in (spiritual) darkness*, that the day should overtake you like a thief; for you are all sons of light and sons of day. We are not of night nor of darkness; so then *let us not sleep as others do* , but be alert and sober.

"For those who sleep do their sleeping at night (in spiritual darkness), and those who get drunk get drunk at night (by stumbling in spiritual darkness). But since we are of the day, let us be sober, having put on (the weapons of our warfare) the breastplate of faith and love, and as a helmet, the hope of salvation. *For God has not destined us for wrath (and judgment), but for obtaining salvation through our Lord Jesus Christ"* (I Thess. 5:4-9).

5

The Harlot Church Today

God's Word warns: "... In the last days difficult times will come. ... Evil men and imposters (false teachers) will proceed from bad to worse, *deceiving and being deceived*. Holding to a *form of godliness* ... avoid such men as these." They "... will be lovers of self (flesh), lovers of money (greed), boastful, arrogant ... unholy, unloving (hating their neighbor) ... gossips (who speak curses), without self-control ... haters of good ... conceited ... *always learning and never able to come to the knowledge of the truth (spiritually blind)*." These men "... *oppose the truth*, men of depraved mind, *rejected as regards the faith*." (II Tim. 3:1, 13, 5, 2-4, 7, 8).

Man-centered religion today thinks it is manifesting the love of God while at the same time it loves and indulges the selfish flesh.

This is doublemindedness. Those caught up in this are not being led by the Spirit of God or they would put to death the deeds of the flesh (Rom. 8:13, 14). They are trying to manifest the love of God through the works of the flesh. All works of the flesh are cursed. This is why these works are called a form of godliness. They can never conform you to the image of Jesus.

The opposite of this, of course, is to preach the whole gospel, and the whole gospel will tell flesh to die. This is not a popular message and will not please men but it is what God's men will do as they seek the approval of God rather than of men. The whole gospel produces holy men and women, (I Pet. 1:14-16; Col. 1:21, 22; and Eph. 5:27, 26).

Since grace has been perverted by false teaching, love is also perverted. The love expressed in most of the church today is just like the world. They hate their neighbor as they slander, condemn, judge, and curse one another. God calls this influence of the world in the church "harlotry" "... For all of them are *adulterers*, an assembly of treacherous men. 'And they bend their tongue like their bow; lies and not truth prevail in the land; ... and *they do not know Me,*' declares the Lord" (Jer. 9:2, 3).

When this congregation assembles, they speak against one another: " 'Let everyone be on guard against his neighbor, and do not trust any brother; because every brother deals craftily, and every neighbor goes about as a slanderer. And everyone deceives his neighbor, and does not speak the truth ... your dwelling is in the midst of deceit; through (walking after the lusts of) deceit they refuse to know Me,' declares the Lord. 'Their tongue is a deadly arrow; it speaks deceit; with his mouth one speaks peace to his neighbor, but inwardly (in his heart) he sets an ambush for him' " (Jer. 9:4-6, 8).

This is so descriptive of the church today. It is as if Jeremiah had written this after seeing the condition in the average church today. This manifestation of the flesh nature of Satan has not changed since the time of Jeremiah. What a form of godliness was then, a form of godliness is today. We must recognize the seriousness of this problem. God calls it harlotry.

James warned: "Do not speak against one another, brethren. He who speaks against a brother, or judges his brother, speaks against the law, and judges the law;

but if you judge the law, *you are not a doer of the law ...*"
(James 4:11).

When we continue to walk after the flesh, we speak
against one another. Instead of being a doer of the law, we
pass judgment on God's law, which in turn brings judgment
on us. A form of godliness totally misses God by producing
a double-minded harlot who speaks blessings and curses
because she wants to walk with Jesus and the flesh nature of
Satan at the same time. This is the result of doctrines that do
not conform you to godliness.

When the love of the flesh nature is removed from your
heart by the washing of the Word of God, your mind no
longer stays on yourself but on how you can love and help
your neighbor. Your mouth bears the fruit of this love. You
are no longer married to the old man (flesh nature). You
have a new husband; his name is Christ. He has all your
heart. This is how you become the bride of Christ.

We are free from the judgment of the law because we
have become a doer of the law and we bear fruit (the fruit of
love) for God. Before we became the bride of Christ, we
were the bride of the old man and we were bearing fruit for
death because we were lawbreakers. Therefore, as the bride
of Christ, we must put to death the old man.

Paul said, "... I died to the Law, that I might live to
God. I have been crucified with Christ (by putting to death
the flesh nature); and it is no longer I who live, but Christ
(who) lives in me ..." (Gal. 2:19, 20).

Paul describes an adulteress in Romans 7: "Therefore
... you ... were made to *die to the Law* (when you die to the
flesh, you die to the law) through the body of Christ, that
you might be joined to another, to Him (Jesus Christ) who
was raised from the dead, that we might bear (the) fruit (of
love) for God. For while we *were in the flesh*, the sinful
passions (the works of the flesh), which were aroused by
the Law, (when Paul saw the law, then he saw his sin
nature) were at work in the members of our body *to bear
fruit for death* (by breaking God's laws). But now we have

been released from the Law, having died to that (old man and flesh nature) by which we were (married and) bound, so that we (now) serve in newness of the Spirit (by being led by the Spirit of God to be perfected in love) and not in oldness of the letter" (Rom. 7:4-6).

Paul explained that the old man must die so that we can be released from the law. The Spirit of God must control our lives to put this flesh nature to death so we can become doers of the law and bear fruit for God. If your heart is married to Christ, you will bear fruit for God. If your heart is still married to the old man, you will bear fruit for Satan.

Paul continues: "Or do you not know, brethren ... that *the law has jurisdiction over a person as long as he lives* (in flesh rebellion)? For the married woman (the bride of the old man) is bound by law (under the judgment of the law) to her husband (the old man and cursed nature) *while he is* (still) *living;* but if her husband (old man) dies (by putting the flesh nature to death), she is released from the law (fulfilled the law and is no longer under the judgment of the law) concerning the husband (the old man). So then if while her husband is living (by continuing to walk after the flesh nature), she is joined to another man (by also trying to walk double-minded as the bride of Christ), *SHE SHALL BE CALLED AN ADULTERESS;* but if her husband (the fleshly old man) dies, she is free from the law (and no longer under the judgment of the law), so that she is not an adulteress, though she is joined to another man (the Lord Jesus Christ)" (Rom. 7:1-3).

An adulteress is anyone who tries to follow Jesus while they still love and walk after the flesh. These scriptures are hidden from those who follow a form of godliness because they are totally contrary to their carnal doctrines. The understanding of these scriptures will become much clearer as we continue in this chapter.

Jesus says, "Therefore you are to be perfect, as your heavenly Father is perfect" (Matt. 5:48).

We become perfect when we no longer speak against our neighbor: "... If anyone does not *stumble in what he says, he is a perfect man,* able to bridle the whole body as well" (James 3:2). "... The tongue is a fire, the very world of iniquity ... and with it we curse men (hate, anger, slander, against our neighbor) ... from the same mouth come both blessing and cursing (double-mindedness). My brethren, *these things ought not to be this way.* This wisdom is not that which comes down from above, but is earthly (when we walk and talk like the world), natural (the flesh nature), demonic (because we do not resist the flaming missiles of the powers of darkness who continually fill our minds with opposition toward our neighbors as they do the world). For where jealousy and *selfish ambition* exist, there is disorder and every evil thing" (James 3:6, 9, 10, 15, 16).

When a congregation follows a doctrine that does not conform them to godliness, they will bless God as they continue to break God's law by speaking curses against their neighbor. This is the double-minded adulteress which we saw in Romans 7: *"YOU ADULTERESSES* (harlot church), do you not know that friendship with the world (when you continue to walk and talk like the world) is hostility toward God? Therefore whoever wishes to be a friend of the world (by being like the world) makes himself an enemy of God" (James 4:4).

A person controlled by worldly wisdom is in rebellion to God and controlled by the powers of darkness: "For let not that man expect that he will receive anything from the Lord, being a double-minded man, unstable in all his ways" (James 1:7, 9).

Doctrines that teach a form of godliness produce a people with selfish ambition who are lovers of themselves: "You lust (by following your fleshly desires) and (you) do not have (your way); so you commit murder (by speaking against your neighbor). And you are *envious* ... so you fight and quarrel (against your neighbor) ... You ask (pray) and *do not receive, because you ask (pray) WITH WRONG MOTIVES ...*" (James 4:2, 3).

Since this congregation still walks after the flesh, they pray for God to cooperate with them while they fulfill selfish ambition by building a self-image and name for themselves. They still love the cursed nature more than Christ. Their prayers are not answered.

The opposite of this is the body of Christ which walks in love. Jesus said: "You did not choose Me, but I chose you, and appointed you, that you should go and bear (the) fruit (of love), and that your *fruit should remain, that whatever you ask of the Father in My name, He may give to you* (God answers all of his prayers because his motive is to walk in love). If you were of the world, the world would love its own ... but I chose you out of the world, therefore the world hates you (because you will not participate with the world in slander, gossip, faultfinding, etc.)" (John 15:16, 19).

If you love the selfish flesh nature more than Christ, you will not lay down your life to walk in love. You will not endure sound doctrine. You will want your ears tickled by false teachers and carnal doctrines: "For the time will come when they *will not endure sound doctrine;* but wanting to have their ears tickled (by pleasing the flesh nature), they will accumulate for themselves teachers in accordance to their own desires (of the flesh); and *will turn away their ears from the truth* (to a false security so they can be lovers of self, lovers of money, boastful, arrogant, unloving, gossips, and haters of good) ..." (II Tim. 4:3, 4).

Everyone makes a choice either to love their life after the nature of Satan or to lay down their life for their neighbor. Those who follow a *form* of godliness remain in darkness, unable to come to the knowledge of the truth, because they do not walk in love: "The one who loves his brother abides (continues) in the light and there is no cause for *stumbling* in him. But the one who hates his brother (by walking after his selfish flesh) is in the darkness, and does not know where he is going because the darkness has blinded his eyes" (I John 2:10, 11).

The powers of darkness bring this darkness which blinds congregations to the true gospel: "... If our gospel is veiled, it is veiled to those who are *perishing*, in whose case the god of this world has blinded the minds of the unbelieving, that they might *not see the light of the gospel* ..." (II Cor. 4:3, 4).

Everyone who chooses to continue to walk after the flesh nature is blinded and destroyed by the powers of darkness.

Listen to the words of Peter: "Therefore, since Christ has suffered in the flesh, arm yourselves also with the same purpose, because he who *has suffered in the flesh has ceased from sin*" (I Peter 4:1). Those who walk after carnal doctrines ignore scriptures such as these. Carnal doctrines do not teach you to put to death the flesh nature. They encourage you to practice sin.

Carnal doctrines and carnal traditions teach congregations to do fleshly works for God instead of taking up their cross and denying their flesh. They make a futile attempt to perfect a fleshly congregation in love after the strength and the works of the flesh. They are accursed because they practice lawlessness (lawbreakers). These doctrines have distorted the gospel and have made the gospel contrary to the truth to fulfill the selfish ambition of men who love their flesh rather than pleasing God. This congregation is at "ease in Zion" because they live for themselves. They refuse to suffer in the flesh in order to cease from sin.

People have turned from God and left their first love by the millions to follow after false teachers and distorted gospels. They know that they do not have the same relationship with Christ that they once had but they do not understand why.

The problem is very simple: "... If any man is preaching to you a gospel contrary to that which you received, let him be accursed" (Gal. 1:9).

This is the falling away and the law removes the hedge and brings judgment against all who teach a doctrine contrary to the glorious gospel of love. You have to die to selfishness in order to walk in love.

The law was not made for a righteous man but to judge the lawless and every teaching and doctrine contrary to the gospel.

Paul wrote: "Realizing the fact that *LAW IS NOT MADE FOR A RIGHTEOUS MAN*, but for those who are *lawless* and rebellious, for the ungodly and sinners, for the unholy ... and whatever else is *CONTRARY* to sound teaching, *ACCORDING TO THE GLORIOUS GOSPEL* ..." (I Tim. 1:9-11).

The law brings judgment, a curse, and the wrath of God on all who participate in a distorted gospel because they are not protected by God.

Paul warned them: "... Instruct certain men not to teach *strange doctrines* ... which give rise to mere speculation rather than furthering the administration of God ... But the goal of our instruction (the true gospel) is *love from a PURE HEART* ... For some men, straying from these things (to another doctrine), have turned aside to fruitless discussion, wanting to be teachers of the Law, even though they do not understand either what they are saying or the matters about which they make confident assertions" (I Tim. 1:3-7).

Paul also cautioned: "If anyone advocates (preaches or teaches) a *different doctrine,* and does not agree with sound words (the gospel), those of our Lord Jesus Christ, and with *the doctrine (gospel) conforming (you) to godliness* (the image of Jesus), he is conceited and *understands nothing;* (because he is ever learning and never able to come to the knowledge of the truth) ..." (I Tim. 6:3, 4). Paul also said: "... in later times some will *FALL AWAY FROM THE*

FAITH, paying attention to deceitful spirits and *doctrines of demons,* " (I Tim. 4:1). This is the falling away.

These doctrines were developed by men who loved selfish ambition. The powers of darkness have deceived these men into taking parts of the Bible to build their doctrines which have captured the hearts of people while fulfilling their selfish ambition. They divide the body of Christ into fleshly kingdoms as they lead congregations into double-mindedness, rebellion, and destruction. They do not build up the body of Christ to the unity of the faith, to a mature man, to the fullness of Christ. This is the adulteress which leads people to draw near to God with their mouths while their hearts still love the nature of Satan. They are not perfected in love. They do not love their neighbor but curse their neighbor.

Matthew wrote in the gospel: " '... The things (words) that proceed out of the mouth come from the heart, and those defile the man' " (Matt. 15:18). Mark wrote: " '... From within, *out of the heart* of men, proceed (from their mouth) ... fornications, thefts, murders, adulteries, deeds of coveting and wickedness, as well as deceit, sensuality, envy, slander, pride, and foolishness' " (Mark 7:21, 22). This is the fruit produced by a form of godliness and the carnal doctrines of men. The doctrines of men will never change the heart. This is the harlot church.

Mark also wrote: " '... This people honors Me with their lips (words) but *their heart* is far away from Me (double-minded). But *IN VAIN* do they worship Me (they are lost), *teaching as doctrines the precepts* (and opinions) *of men. Neglecting the commandment of God, you* hold to the (carnal) *tradition of men ... you nicely set aside the commandment of God in order to keep your tradition. Thus invalidating the word of God (making it of no effect) by your* tradition which you have handed down ...' " (Mark 7:6-9, 13). This is what the carnal doctrines of men have done to congregations today. They produce a deceitful form of godliness.

In the book of Titus we read: "... To those who are defiled and unbelieving, nothing is pure, but both their mind and their conscience are defiled. They profess to know God, but by their deeds they deny Him, being detestible and disobedient, and *worthless* for any good deed" (Titus 1:15, 16).

Listen to the word of the great prophet: "Behold, you are trusting in deceptive words to no avail. Will you steal, murder, and commit adultery, and swear falsely, and offer sacrifices to Baal (idols), and walk after other gods that you have not known, then come and stand before Me in this house, which is called by My name, and say, 'WE ARE DELIVERED!' ... Has this house, which is called by My name, become a den of robbers ...?" (Jer. 7:8-11). "... This is what I commanded them, saying, 'Obey My voice, and I will be your God, and you will be My people; and you will walk in all the way which I command you, that it may be well with you.'

"Yet they did not obey or incline their ear, but walked in their *own counsels* and in the *stubbornness of their evil heart,* and went backward and not forward (and did not overcome). And you shall speak all these words to them, *but they will not listen to you;* and you shall call to them, but they will not answer you. And you shall say to them, 'This is the nation that did not obey the voice (Word) of the Lord their God or *accept correction* (reproof and discipline); truth has perished and has been cut off from their mouth (famine of the Word)" (Jer. 7:23, 24, 27, 28).

Then the prophet added: "And the (spiritually) dead bodies of this people will be food for the birds of the sky, and for the beasts of the earth (hedge is removed to the powers of darkness); and no one will frighten them away. Then I will *make to cease* from the cities of Judah and from the streets of Jerusalem (the church) the *voice of joy* and the *voice of gladness,* the *voice of the bridegroom* (Jesus) and the *voice of the bride* (the body of Christ); for the land will become a ruin (cursed)" (Jer. 7:33, 34).

These scriptures perfectly describe the spiritual darkness and destruction which is on the harlot church today. Yet the harlot is offended when you attempt to show her the truth because she is wise in her own eyes.

Isaiah also addressed this issue: "Then the Lord said, 'Because this people draw near with their words and *honor Me with lip service, but they remove their hearts far from Me,* and *their reverence* for Me consists of *TRADITION* learned by rote (repetition), for the Lord has poured over you a *spirit of deep sleep* (curse), He has shut your eyes (in sleep), the prophets; and He has covered your heads, the seers (in spiritual darkness)" (Isa. 29:13, 10). "And the *ENTIRE VISION* (of God's Word) shall be to you like the *WORDS OF A SEALED BOOK* (no understanding) ... And the (fleshly) wisdom of their wise men shall perish, and *THE DISCERNMENT OF THEIR DISCERNING MEN SHALL BE CONCEALED* (with no comprehension of the powers of darkness in their midst)" (Isa. 29:11, 14).

Hear the words of Hosea: "... For the Lord has a case against the inhabitants of the land, because there is no faithfulness or kindness ... There is swearing, deception, murder, stealing, and adultery ... *Let no one find fault* (compromise), and *let none offer reproof* (or discipline) ... so you will stumble by day, and the prophet also will stumble with you by night (in spiritual darkness); and I will destroy your mother (the church). My people are destroyed for lack of knowledge. Because you have rejected knowledge, I also will reject you from being My priest ..." (Hosea 4:1, 2, 4-6).

Hosea also wrote: "... For now, O Ephraim, you have *played the harlot,* Israel has *defiled* itself. Their deeds (works of the flesh) will not allow them to return to their God. For a *spirit of harlotry* is within them, and *they do not know the Lord.* They have dealt treacherously against the Lord ... *they have borne illegitimate children* (false sons). ... Ephraim is oppressed, crushed in judgment (the congregation is cursed), because he was determined *to follow man's command*. Therefore I am like a *moth* to Ephraim, and like *rotteness* to the house of Judah (the hedge is removed for the powers of darkness). For I will be like a lion to Ephraim, and like a young lion to the house of Judah. I, even I, will tear to pieces and go away, I will carry away, and there will be none to deliver. I will go away and return to My place (the presence of God is gone) until they acknowledge their guilt and see My face ..." (Hosea 5:3, 4, 7, 11, 12, 14, 15).

Because of His abundant grace, God is shining a light today in Jerusalem (the church). The wise (virgins) will come to the light and be perfected in love. The foolish (virgins), the harlot church, will scoff and mock with controversial questions and disputes about words.

God is saying to this harlot church today: "Wash your heart from evil, O Jerusalem, that you may be saved. How long will your wicked thoughts lodge within you? How long must I see the standard (of the Word of God), and hear the sound of the trumpet (warning of judgment)? For My people are *FOOLISH* (virgins), they *know Me not;* they are stupid children, and they have *no understanding*. They are shrewd to do evil, but to do good they do not know" (Jer. 4:14, 21, 22).

Everyone who sins against God dies. Therefore God, through His mercy and grace, has made a provision for us to be forgiven through Jesus Christ and the blood of the cross. Jesus became a sacrifice so that our rebellious acts against God could be forgiven. When we are forgiven, the powers of darkness lose their hold on our lives because we are removed from God's judgment against sin.

Everyone who does not walk in the way of God is being destroyed by the powers of darkness. With each deed of rebellion against God or his neighbor, the powers of darkness get ground to bring punishment and destruction. When we come to God and turn from the selfish ways of the world to walk in the loving ways of God — this is covenant.

But how do we walk in the ways of God when, like the world, we have only known the selfish ways of Satan? This is the reason Jesus came, not only as a sacrifice for our sins, but to show us how we should walk. Even more, He brought a book of instruction called the Word of God and His Spirit to counsel us so that we can be reconciled back to God. This book explains a way of life which is totally foreign to the people of the world. This book gives us instructions on how we are to be perfected in love so that we may be reconciled to God.

We have to know what God requires or we would not know how to walk. This is called understanding. As we read the Word of God, the Spirit of God counsels us and shows us the things we must turn from and the things we must do in order to please God. The Spirit of God leads us to overcome all the ways of Satan so that we no longer walk and talk like the selfish world. Our minds are renewed to walk and talk like God. We are no longer conformed to the former lusts of the flesh, but we learn to become holy like Jesus in all our behaviour. We are conformed to the image of Jesus and escape the corruption that is in the world by lust.

Because we no longer live for ourselves, we are reconciled back to God, a new creation. Old things have passed away. As Jesus Christ walked in this world, so do we. As ambassadors of God, we take this word to others that they also may be delivered from judgment and be reconciled back to God.

Like Jesus, we forsake selfish ambition and gain of this world because our citizenship is now in heaven. The real treasure on this earth is to please God and receive His love and blessings which far exceed anything this earth can offer.

What do we do if we make a mistake and break God's law? When we break God's law, the powers of darkness move, to attack us, and we lose our peace. To a Christian this is reproof and discipline from God because a Christian is supposed to walk in peace with a hedge around him. If he no longer has peace, he knows he has broken God's law which has removed this hedge and given ground to the powers of darkness. Because of God's provision through Jesus Christ at Calvary, he has a place of repentance so that the judgment of this sin may be removed. Therefore, when he repents by turning from this sin, he is no longer a lawbreaker and the hedge and peace return.

If we do not continue to walk in peace and obedience, the powers of darkness are able to get more ground until we are destroyed. Therefore, everyone who does not walk in covenant is being destroyed by the powers of darkness. By walking in covenant, we keep God's law and receive protection from destruction. Only those who walk in repentance and covenant will survive the destruction of the powers of darkness on this earth today.

When we receive God's knowledge and understanding, we learn the fear of God and the judgment of God: "The fear of the Lord is the beginning of knowledge ..." (Prov. 1:7).

If we have not learned the fear of God, we obviously have not learned the wisdom and knowledge of God. If someone does not have understanding, he is blind to the judgment and wrath of God today. When people do not have a true knowledge of God's judgments, they become arrogant and hostile toward God like the sleeping church today.

This world literally becomes a testing ground to see if we are worthy of heaven. If we receive God's instruction, we will overcome the judgment of this world by being perfected in the love and the nature of God. It is a natural thing to overcome when we love the Lord with all our hearts, because all our motives will be to please God.

The result of this obedience is to have the nature of God. However, if we choose to walk in selfishness, like Satan, we have made a choice to go to the same judgment as Satan. Therefore, everyone who does not submit and receive this wisdom from God is slowly destroyed.

A wise man will seek the wisdom and protection of God through walking in covenant. Of course, the wisdom of God comes only through Jesus Christ "... who became to us wisdom from God ..." (I Cor. 1:30). Since Jesus and the Word are the same, Jesus and the Word of God are the wisdom that was sent from God to rescue and *SAVE US* from death and destruction. This is the gospel that Jesus brought to us from heaven.

God has so written the Word that we must come to Him with all our hearts in order to understand its mystery. With God's knowledge and wisdom, He shows us how to avoid the adulteress and a counterfeit form of godliness which leads people blindly to death and destruction. Throughout Proverbs, God's word describes how we either walk in blessings or curses of God. Jesus is referred to as wisdom and we can see His church as well as the false church of harlotry. She has no understanding of God's laws. Therefore, she has no fear of God. She walks in darkness, death, and destruction.

Jude warns about these last days: "... In the last time there shall be mockers (scoffers and foolish men), following after their own ungodly lusts ... worldly minded, devoid of the Spirit" (Jude 18, 19).

Because a scoffer loves the flesh, he is worldly minded. He walks and talks like the world. He has no understanding of the wisdom of God. He is wise in his own eyes. Unlike the wise man, he refuses the reproof and discipline which he must have to be perfected in love.

We see in Proverbs: "Does not wisdom (Jesus Christ) call, and understanding lift up her voice? To you, O men, I call, and my voice (the Word) is to the sons of men. *Take my instruction,* and not silver, and knowledge rather than choicest gold. For wisdom is better than jewels; and all desirable things cannot compare with her. *The fear of the Lord is to hate evil; pride and arrogance and the evil way, and the perverted mouth, I hate.* Counsel is mine and sound wisdom; I am understanding, power is mine. I love those who love me; and those who diligently seek me will find me. My fruit (of the Spirit) is better than gold, even pure gold, and my yield than choicest silver. I walk in the way of righteousness ... to endow those who love me with wealth, that I may fill their treasuries. *Heed instruction* and *be wise* ... blessed is the man who listens to me ... for he who finds me finds life, and obtains favor from the Lord. But he who sins against me injures himself; all those who hate me love death" (Prov. 8:1, 4, 10, 11, 13, 14, 17, 19-21, 33-36.)

In Proverbs we also read: "Do not reprove a scoffer (who loves the flesh), lest he hate you, reprove a wise man, and he will love you. He who corrects a scoffer gets dishonor for himself, and he who reproves a wicked man (who loves the flesh) gets insults for himself. Give instruction to a wise man, and he will be still wiser, teach a righteous man, and he will increase his learning" (Prov. 9:8, 7, 9).

A scoffer is a harlot who has a form of godliness. She loves the flesh nature and the ways of Satan more than the ways of God.

This is how the harlot church becomes a dwelling place of demons. For this rebellion, she is destroyed by the powers of darkness.

We also find this teaching in Proverbs: "Wisdom (Jesus) shouts in the street ... How long, O naive ones, will you love simplicity? And scoffers (who follow fleshly desires) delight themselves in scoffing, and fools hate knowledge? *Turn to My reproof, behold, I will pour out my spirit on you; I will make my words known to you.* Because I called you, and you refused (to walk in love); I stretched out my hand, and no one paid attention; and you neglected all my counsel, and did not want my reproof ... I will mock when your *dread comes,* when your dread (the powers of darkness) comes like a storm, and your calamity comes on like a whirlwind, when distress and anguish come on you. Because they hated knowledge, and did not choose (to learn) the fear of the Lord ... they spurned all my reproof. So they shall eat of the fruit of their own way ... the complacency of fools shall destroy them. But he who listens to me shall live securely, and shall be at ease (and protected) from the *dread of evil*" (Prov. 1:20, 22-27, 29-33).

Proverbs continues: "My son, if you will receive my sayings ... make your ear attentive to wisdom, incline your heart to understanding; if you seek her (with all your heart) as silver, and search for her as for hidden treasures; *then you will discern the fear of the Lord,* and discover the knowledge of God. For the Lord gives wisdom; from His mouth (the Word of God) come knowledge and understanding ... He is a shield (hedge) to those who walk in integrity (covenant) ... and He preserves the way of His godly ones" (Prov. 2:1, 2, 4-8).

"For (God's) wisdom will enter your heart ... discretion will guard you, understanding will watch over you, to deliver you from the way of evil, from the man (harlot) who speaks perverse things (perverts the Word); from those (harlots) who leave the paths of uprightness, to walk in the ways of (fleshly) darkness; to deliver you from the strange woman (harlot), from the *adulteress* who flatters with her words; *that leaves the companion of her youth (Jesus Christ),* and forgets the covenant of her God (by turning her ears from the truth); for her house sinks down to death, and *her tracks lead to the dead;* none who go to her return again, nor do they reach the paths of life. So you will walk in the way of good men, and keep to the paths of the righteous. For the upright will live (and be protected) in the land ... but the wicked will be cut off (and destroyed) from the land ..." (Prov. 2:10-13, 16-22).

These scriptures show us the church Jesus Christ builds and the false church the harlot builds. The harlot church is a synagogue of Satan (Rev. 2:9). The church that Jesus Christ builds is wisdom: "Wisdom has built her house, she has hewn out her seven pillars; she has prepared her food (the Word of God), she has mixed her wine (the teaching); she has also set her table (covenant); she has sent out her maidens (the body of Christ) ... 'Whoever is naive, *let him TURN IN HERE!'* To him who lacks understanding she says, 'Come eat of my food (Word), and drink of the wine (teaching) I have mixed. Forsake your folly (lusts) and live, and proceed in the way of understanding.' For by me your days will be multiplied, and years of life will be added to you" (Prov. 9:1-6, 11).

If we become a part of the house Jesus builds, we will have the covenant protection of God to protect us from the powers of darkness. This is how our days will be multiplied and the years of life will be added to us because we fulfill God's law: "My son, do not forget my teaching, *but let your heart keep My commandments;* for length of days and years of life, and peace (and protection) they will add to you. Do not be wise (after the flesh) in your own eyes; fear the Lord and turn away from evil ... Do not reject the discipline of the Lord ... for whom the Lord loves He reproves ..." (Prov. 3:1, 2, 7, 11, 12).

The wise virgins make up the body of Christ. The foolish virgins are the harlot church. She is without understanding, having no fear of God, wise in her own eyes. She is ever learning, never able to come to the knowledge of truth.

The scripture describes her as the (foolish) woman of folly: "... She is naive, and knows nothing. And she sits at the doorway of her house (the false church) ... calling to those who pass by, who are making their paths straight: 'Whoever is naive, *LET HIM TURN IN HERE*' ... but he does not know that the dead are there, that her guests are in the depths of Sheol" (Prov. 9:13-16, 18). "With her *many persuasions* she entices him; with her flattering lips she seduces him (through fleshly desires). Suddenly he follows her, as an ox goes to the slaughter, or as one in fetters to the discipline of a fool, until an arrow (the powers of darkness) pierces through his liver; as a bird hastens to the snare, so *he does not know that it will cost him his life*" (Prov. 7:21-23).

Proverbs continues: "Do not let your heart turn aside to her ways, do not stray into her paths. For *many are the victims* she has cast down, and *numerous are all her slain.*

Her house is the way to Sheol, descending to the chambers of death" (Prov. 7:25-27). "My son, do not forget my teaching, but let your heart keep my commandments; for length of days and years of life, and peace they will add to you. Trust in the Lord with all your heart, and do not lean on your own understanding. My son, do not reject the discipline of the Lord (to perfect you in love) ... for whom the Lord loves He reproves, even as a father, the son in whom he delights. Do not be wise in your own eyes; fear the Lord and turn away from evil" (Prov. 3:1, 2, 5, 11, 12, 7).

"For the lips (words) of an *adulteress* drip honey, and smoother than oil is her speech; *her feet go down to death, her steps lay hold of Sheol.* She does not ponder the path of life; her ways are unstable, SHE DOES NOT KNOW IT ... Do not go near the door of her house, lest you give your vigor (strength) to others, and *your years to the cruel one* (Satan); lest strangers (the powers of darkness) be filled with your strength ... and you groan at your latter end (with sickness), when your flesh and your body are consumed; and you say, 'How I have hated instruction! And my heart spurned reproof! *I was almost in utter ruin in the midst of the (adulterous assembly) and congregation'* " (Prov. 5:3, 5, 6, 8-12, 14). This is where thousands are finding themselves today.

"For the ways of a man are before the eyes of the Lord, and He watches all his paths. His own iniquities will capture the wicked, and he will be held with the cords of his sin. *He will die for lack of instruction,* and in ... his folly he will *go astray"* (Prov. 5:21-23).

"Do not enter the path of the wicked ... avoid it ... TURN AWAY from it and pass on. For they eat the bread (words) of wickedness, and drink the wine (teaching) of violence. But the path of the righteous ... shines brighter and brighter until the full day. *The way of the wicked (harlot) is like darkness* (spiritual darkness); they do not know over what they stumble ... let your heart hold fast my words; keep my commandments and live ... for they are *life* to those who find them, and *health* to all their whole body. Watch over your heart with all diligence, for from it flow the springs (fruit) of life" (Prov. 4:14, 15, 17-19, 4, 22, 23).

"*Give me your heart, my son, and let your eyes delight in my ways.* For a *harlot* is a deep pit, and an *adulterous woman* is a narrow well. Surely she lurks as a robber, and *increases the faithless among men* (by teaching rebellious people that they are righteous)" (Prov. 23:26-28).

The Psalmist wrote: "But to the wicked God says, 'What right have you to tell of My statutes, and to take My covenant in your mouth? For you hate discipline, and you cast My words behind you. When you see a thief, you are pleased with him, and you associate with adulterers. You let your mouth loose in evil (by speaking curses), and your tongue frames deceit (because you love selfishness). You sit and speak against your brother. You slander your own mother's son. These things you have done, and I kept silence; *YOU THOUGHT I WAS JUST LIKE YOU ...*" (Ps. 50:16-21).

"For My people have committed two evils. They have forsaken Me, *the fountain of living waters,* to hew for themselves cisterns (religious systems), broken cisterns, that can hold no water (because the Word can have no place in them). The young lions (powers of darkness) have roared at him, they have roared loudly. And they have made his land a waste. His cities (churches) have been destroyed without (spiritual) inhabitant. Have you not done this to yourself, by your forsaking the Lord your God ... but now what are you doing on the *road to Egypt* (the world) ..." (Jer. 2:13, 15, 17, 18). "Can a virgin forget her ornaments, or a bride her attire? Yet *My people have forgotten Me days without number.* Also on your skirts is found the lifeblood of the innocent poor (the lost); you did not find them breaking in ..." (Jer. 2:32, 34).

Jeremiah also said: "Therefore the showers (Holy Spirit) have been withheld, and there has been no spring rain (for revival). Yet you had a *harlot's forehead;* you refused to (repent and) be ashamed" (Jer. 3:3).

Zephaniah said: "This is the exultant city (proud church) which *dwells securely* (with a false security) ... how she has become a desolation, a resting place for beasts (a dwelling place of demons)! Everyone who passes by her will hiss and wave his hand in contempt (as it is today). Woe to her who is rebellious and defiled, the tyrannical city (church)! She heeded no voice, she accepted no instruction (discipline). She did not trust in the Lord; she did not draw near to her God" (Zeph. 2:15; 3:1, 2).

Hosea said: *"For Israel has forgotten his Maker and built palaces ...* but I will send *fire* on its cities that it may consume its palacial dwellings ... for you have played the harlot forsaking your God ..."* (Hosea 8:14; 9:1).

Listen to the words of Amos: " 'The songs of the palace will turn to wailing in that day,' declares the Lord God. *'Many will be the corpses; in every place they will cast them forth in silence.'* 'And it will come about in that day,' declares the Lord God, 'that I shall make the sun go down at noon (in spiritual darkness) in broad daylight. Then I shall turn your festivals (church activities) into mourning and all your songs into lamentation ...' " (Amos 8:3, 9, 10).

Again, Jeremiah said: " 'Therefore behold, I am against the prophets ... who steal my words (or sermons) from each other. Behold, I am against the prophets,' declares the Lord, 'who use their tongues and declare, 'The Lord declares.' 'Behold, I am against those who have prophesied false dreams,' declares the Lord, 'and related them, and led my people astray by their falsehoods (carnal traditions) and *reckless boasting;* yet I did not send them or command them, nor do they furnish this people the slightest benefit,' declares the Lord" (Jer. 23:30-32).

The Apostle Paul wrote: *"Beware* of the dogs (those outside the covenant), *beware* of the evil workers, *beware* of the false circumcision (the false church); for we are the true circumcision (the true church), who worship in the Spirit of

God and *glory in Christ Jesus* (not in men and doctrines) and *put no confidence in the flesh.* For many walk, of whom I often told you, and now tell you even weeping, that they are *enemies of the cross of Christ,* whose end is destruction ... who set their minds on *earthly things.* For our *citizenship is in heaven,* from which also we *eagerly wait* for a Saviour, the Lord Jesus Christ" (Phil. 3:2, 3, 18-20).

Paul also said: "See to it that no one takes you captive through *philosophy* (intellect and academics) and *empty deception* (lust of deceit), according to the *traditions of men* (carnal doctrines), according to the elementary *principles of the world* (doing the work of God through the strength of the flesh and using worldly methods), rather than according to (the true gospel of) Christ. As you therefore have received Christ Jesus the Lord, *so walk in Him"* (Col. 2:8, 6).

The Psalmist said: "Those who hate the Lord would pretend obedience to Him and their time of punishment would be forever" (Ps. 81:15). "Examine me, O Lord, and try me; test my mind and my heart. I do not sit with *deceitful men,* nor will I go with *pretenders.* I hate the assembly of *evildoers,* and I will not sit with the wicked" (Ps. 26:2, 4, 5).

6

The Prophets of Old Spoke of These Days

Some Jews in Rome came to Paul to hear his view about the gospel of the Lord Jesus Christ: "And when they had set a day for him, they came to him at his lodging in large numbers; and he was explaining to them ... about the kingdom of God, and trying to persuade them concerning Jesus from both the *law of Moses* and from the *prophets* ..." (Acts 28:23).

Just as the teaching from the law and the prophets applied to the days of Paul, the law and the prophets teach us about these last days.

We saw a very good example of this when Paul referred to God's wrath and destruction on the children of Israel in the wilderness. Paul said these things happened as an *example for us today:* "Now these things happened to them *as an example,* and *they were written for our instruction, upon whom the ends of the ages have come"* (I Cor. 10:11).

The apostles saw clearly that the messages in the prophets were not simply an historical record, but a vital message for our day. Again, we are told: "For whatever was written in earlier times was *written for our instruction* ..." (Rom. 15:4).

Jesus, after He was resurrected, made reference to the law of Moses, the prophets, and Psalms, to His disciples: "And He said to them, 'O foolish men and slow of heart to believe in all that the prophets have spoken!' And beginning with Moses and all the prophets, He explained the things concerning Himself in all the scriptures ... He said to them, 'These are My words which I spoke to you while I was with you that all things which are written about Me in the *law of Moses* and *the prophets* and *the Psalms* must be *fulfilled*" (Luke 24:25, 27, 44).

The prophecy about Jesus was being fulfilled in those days when He went to Calvary. It is no different today as the law of Moses, the prophets, and Psalms are still teaching us about this day we are living in and the coming of the Lord.

Peter said about the prophets: "As to this salvation, the prophets who prophesied of the grace that would come to you made careful search and inquiry ... *It was revealed to them that they were not serving themselves* (their generation), *BUT YOU,* in these things which now have been announced to you through those who preached the gospel to you ..." (I Pet. 1:10, 12).

Both the major and minor prophets are filled with scriptures about this time of judgment which has come upon us today.

Tunnel vision has blinded us to this part of the Word of God as we have been blinded to the fear of God. The New Testament clearly instructs us to go back to the prophets to have understanding about God's judgment during these days.

Peter also made reference to a statement made by Moses about the judgment of these last days: "Moses said ... 'To Him (Jesus) you shall *give heed in everything He says to you.* And it shall be that *every soul that does not heed that prophet (Christ) shall be UTTERLY DESTROYED from among the people* (this judgment comes at the hands of the powers of darkness who fulfill the curse). And likewise, *ALL THE PROPHETS WHO HAVE SPOKEN, FROM SAMUEL AND HIS SUCCESSORS ONWARD, ALSO ANNOUNCED THESE DAYS* (of judgment and destruction)" (Acts 3:22-24).

Peter confirmed that *ALL THE PROPHETS* from Samuel onward are warning about these last days.

Part of the reason the law has been lost today is because carnal doctrines have taught that the prophets of old are only for historical revelation. The sleeping church today sighs in relief, saying that it sure is nice to live in this "age of grace" when God does not discipline or expect His people to obey Him anymore.

However, the Lord still expects His people to be "holy and blameless." It becomes increasingly easier to skip scriptures when you have a false security and a hardened heart.

Instead of our ancestors heeding these warnings and walking in obedience to the Word of God, they passed on to us misleading doctrines of "peace and safety" for these last days.

The book of Acts records the apostles and disciples of the early church faithfully preaching the whole message of the prophets to the people of their day: "Take heed therefore, *so that THE THING SPOKEN OF IN THE PROPHETS (about the judgments of the powers of darkness) may not come upon you;* 'Behold, you scoffers (who follow flesh), and marvel, and *perish;* for I am accomplishing a work in your days, a work which *you will never believe, though someone should describe it to you'* " (Acts 13:40, 41). The fallen-away church is offended today when you try to explain about the powers of darkness in their midst.

Those who walk after the flesh never have understanding about judgment. The people of Paul's day understood that the prophets were not speaking simply historical revelation. They knew these messages were essential warnings for us today. They were describing the destruction which is coming on us today by the powers of darkness.

Let us go to the scripture Paul was referring to: "Look among the nations! *Observe! Be astonished! Wonder!* Because I am doing something in your days — *you would not believe if you were told.* For behold, I am raising up the Chaldeans (powers of darkness), that fierce and impetuous people who march throughout the earth to *seize dwelling places* which are not theirs. They mock at *kings,* and *rulers* are a laughing matter to them. They laugh at every fortress, and heap up rubble to capture it ... *Thou, O Lord, HAST APPOINTED THEM TO JUDGE* (sin); *AND THOU, O ROCK, HAST ESTABLISHED THEM TO CORRECT* (chastise when we break God's law)" (Hab. 1:5, 6, 10, 12).

The Holy Spirit obviously was directing Paul as he spoke this message of warning to the people of his day and is speaking it to us as well.

As you continue in this study of the messages from the prophets to us in these last days, you will be amazed at the accuracy with which the churches and church leaders of today are described.

Jeremiah wrote in Lamentations: "How shall I admonish you? To what shall I compare you, O daughter of Jerusalem? To what shall I liken you as I comfort you, O virgin daughter of Zion? For your ruin is as vast as the sea; *who can heal you? YOUR PROPHETS HAVE SEEN FOR YOU FALSE AND FOOLISH VISIONS* (preaching carnal traditions, peace and safety); and *they have not exposed your iniquity* (of breaking God's laws) so as to *restore you from captivity* (of the powers of darkness), but they have seen for you *false and misleading oracles.*

"The Lord has done what He purposed; He has *accomplished His word* which He commanded from days of old (*the curse*). *He has thrown down* (destroyed) without sparing, and *He has caused* the enemy to rejoice over you; *He has exalted* the might of your adversaries" (Lam. 2:13, 14, 17).

Also in Lamentations we find: "The yoke of my transgression is bound; by His hand they are knit together; they have come upon my neck (bondage); He has made my strength fail; the Lord has given me into the hands of those against whom I am not able to stand. The Lord has rejected all my strong men (after the flesh) in my midst; He has called an appointed time against me to crush my young men; the Lord has trodden as in a winepress the virgin daughter of Judah (the day of the Lord). For these things I weep; my eyes run down with water; because *far from me is a COMFORTER (HOLY SPIRIT), ONE WHO RESTORES MY SOUL;* My children are *desolate because the enemy has prevailed.* I called to my lovers, but they deceived me; my priests (preachers) and my elders *perished* in the city, while they sought food to restore their strength themselves" (Lam. 1:14-16, 19).

"*Her ADVERSARIES have become HER MASTERS,* her enemies prosper; for the Lord has caused her grief because of the multitude of her *transgressions;* her little ones have gone away as *captives* before the *adversary.* Her uncleanness was in her skirts (harlotry with the world); she did not consider her future; therefore she has *FALLEN ASTONISHINGLY* (fallen away from the faith); *she has no comforter* (no Holy Spirit). 'See, O Lord, my affliction, for the enemy has magnified himself!' " (Lam. 1:5, 9).

"Who is there who speaks and it comes to pass, *unless the Lord has commanded it?* Is it not from the mouth of the Most High that both good *(blessings)* and ill *(curses)* go forth? Why should any living mortal, or any man, offer complaint in view of his sins?" (Lam. 3:37-39).

"The Lord has accomplished His wrath, He has poured out His fierce anger; and He has kindled a *fire* in Zion (the church) which has consumed its *foundations* (of carnal traditions). The kings of the earth *DID NOT BELIEVE,* nor did any of the inhabitants of the world, *THAT THE ADVERSARY AND THE ENEMY* (the powers of darkness) *COULD ENTER THE GATES OF JERUSALEM* (the church), *because of the sins of her prophets and the iniquities of her priests* (preachers), who have shed in her midst the *blood of the righteous* (by perverting the Word of God)" (Lam. 4:11-13).

7

False Teachers Today

The gospel of Matthew says: "Beware of false prophets (preachers and teachers) who come to you in sheep's clothing (pretending to be servants of righteousness), but inwardly (in their hearts) are ravenous wolves (deceitful)" (Matt. 7:15).

These false shepherds and teachers are the very opposite of lambs. They flatter congregations with words in order to fulfill their selfish ambitions in the flesh. Their motives are perverted like wolves. Many will follow these teachers in the last days and believe that Jesus is really their Lord. But Jesus will not know them because they bear the fruit of the flesh. A blind teacher led them after carnal doctrines so that they did not act upon the Word of God. Jesus will say: "I never knew you, depart from Me you who practice lawlessness (sin)." (Matt. 7:23).

Many deceived ancestors have developed carnal doctrines which are deceiving people today. These doctrines were developed by men who were blinded to the truth because their hearts loved selfish ambition. When a teacher's heart loves selfish ambition, he will seek the approval of men rather than the approval of God. He will fulfill his selfish ambition through seeking to make a name for himself, a reputation, popularity and approval.

The only root (motive) in a person's heart should be Jesus, not selfish ambition. When any person continues to walk after selfish ambition, he is still walking in rebellion and the flesh. He is not being controlled by the Spirit of God.

If a person has a root of pride and greed in his heart which he will not give up, his motives will be to please himself. He wants to make a name for Jesus after the strength of the flesh, while he *takes a part* of the glory to build a reputation and name for himself — all because his heart loves pride and greed.

Since his motives have become perverted, he will exploit congregations as he builds up his own image and makes a name for himself and his church. Only the rebellious flesh seeks to take for itself part of the glory which belongs to Jesus.

Satan uses false teachers to please men and make them feel secure in their worldly lifestyles. In exchange, Satan sets these teachers up as lords over God's heritage while he fulfills their fleshly ambition. When these fleshly teachers move in as lords over God's heritage, Satan can then move the congregation into darkness and destruction. The powers of darkness cooperate with these blinded flesh kings by keeping the congregations in subjection through fear, intimidation, and guilt.

When the powers of darkness can get a pastor or teacher to love reputation, they can easily keep them from teaching the parts of the Bible that conform the congregation to godliness. Since he needs the approval of the congregation to fulfill his selfish ambition, he will not deal with certain parts of the Bible which will offend their fleshly natures.

He will welcome the thoughts and suggestions of the powers of darkness which tell him how deceitfully to take advantage of the congregations to build his fleshly reputation. At the same time, the powers of darkness are able to get him to water down and back off the Word of God by making him fearful of losing his reputation and his position. They will attack his mind with fear of losing numbers, popularity, approval, big tithers, his job, and the other things that are necessary to fulfill his selfish ambition.

Every pastor and teacher reading this book will recall these threatening thoughts of intimidation that come each time he has ever taught against carnal traditions. These attacks come even while he is preaching or teaching.

Because of selfish ambition, he will skip over, back off, or water down the Word because his motives have become perverted. *The congregation will then receive only a part of the gospel because the gospel has become perverted.* He leads his fleshly congregation to be at ease in Zion. He has a deceived heart.

Men who teach carnal doctrines become kings as they fulfill their own lusts for pride, greed, name, and reputation. They honor men and teach others also to honor men. These false teachers are the instruments Satan uses to lead congregations to destruction by giving them a false security. The powers of darkness then capture the hearts of people while they fulfill the false teacher's selfish ambition. The congregation is then blinded to the real gospel. They are led into a form of godliness and destruction.

People today are in bondage, confusion, torment, and defeat. They are boxed into ungodly structures just like the Pharisees; and like the Pharisees, they cannot understand or hear the words of Jesus because these carnal doctrines and religious traditions have captured their hearts.

Men of the world, and false teachers and preachers in the church, who love pride and greed, always show partiality and exploit their relationships with one another in order to fulfill their selfish ambitions. Selfish flesh always shows partiality and uses people selfishly rather than truly loving them: "... With his mouth one speaks peace to his neighbor, but inwardly (in his heart) he sets an ambush for him" (Jer. 9:8).

This is exactly how Satan has the world, and the world in the church, living for themselves today. People of the world spend their whole lives seeking a name, reputation, career, power, success, and control. Satan has very subtly moved these ways of the world into the church today. You can no longer tell the difference between the methods of the world and the methods of the church. *Their goals are the same* — to make a name for themselves. Each one is seeking his own selfish interests.

Listen to the words of Ezekiel: "And they come to you as people come, and sit before you as My people (pretending to be God's people), and hear your words, but they do not do them, for they do the lustful desires (of the flesh) expressed by their mouth (fruit), and their heart goes after their gain (for the flesh) … They hear your words, but they do not practice them" (Ezek. 33:31, 32).

They will not practice the Word of God because they have been given a false security: "Those who hate the Lord would pretend obedience to Him; and their time of punishment would be forever" (Ps. 81:15).

Jeremiah said: " 'Hear this, O foolish and senseless people, who have eyes, but see not; who have ears, but hear not. Do you not fear Me?' declares the Lord … 'But this people has a stubborn and rebellious heart …' An appalling and horrible thing has happened … the prophets (preachers) prophesy falsely (carnal doctrines), and the priests (kings of pride) rule on their own authority (not God's authority); and My people love it so! But what will you do at the end of it?' " (Jer. 5:21-23, 30, 31). "To whom shall I speak and give warning, that they may hear? Behold, their ears are closed, and they cannot listen. Behold, the word of the Lord has become a reproach (offense) to them; they have no delight in it" (Jer. 6:10).

Paul told the Thessalonians that he preached the gospel amid much opposition from the flesh. He said that all his motives were to please God, not men or himself.

Paul said: "... As you know, we had the boldness in our God to speak to you the gospel of God amid much opposition. For our exhortation does not come from *error* or *impurity* or by *way of deceit;* but just as we have been approved by God to be entrusted with the gospel, so we speak, *not as pleasing men but God,* who examines our hearts. For we never came with *flattering speech,* as you know, nor with a *pretext for greed* ... nor did we seek glory from men ..." (I Thess. 2:2-6).

Paul would not pervert the Word of God to receive the approval of man. He taught the whole counsel of God's Word amid much fleshly opposition.

False teachers who love selfish ambition will not teach the whole counsel of God's Word because their motives are self-centered and they seek the approval of men rather than God. Paul said: "For I did not shrink (back) from declaring to you the whole purpose (whole counsel) of God" (Acts 20:27).

Paul said to the Phillipians: "Some, to be sure, are preaching Christ even from *envy* and *strife,* but some also from good will; the latter do it out of love ... the former proclaim Christ out of *SELFISH AMBITION, rather than from PURE MOTIVES* ..." (Phil. 1:15-17).

Paul was having problems finding a teacher to send to the Phillipians because the teachers all had impure motives and loved selfish ambition. Paul said: "For I have no one else of kindred spirit (who truly seeks the interest of the Lord) who will genuinely be concerned for your welfare (or will not exploit you). *For they all seek after their own interest (pride and greed), not those of Christ Jesus"* (Phil. 2:20, 21).

In Acts, Paul warned the overseers: "Be on guard for yourselves and for all the flock ... I know that after my departure *savage wolves* will come in among you, not sparing the flock; and from among your own selves men will arise, speaking perverse things (perverting the Word), *to draw away the disciples after them* (selfish ambition)."

Paul continued, "... I commend you to God and to the word of His grace, which is able to build you up and *to give you the inheritance among all those who are sanctified"* (Acts 20:28-30, 32).

Those who love selfish ambition cannot lead a congregation to be sanctified. This is why false teachers will lead many in the last days to say, "Lord, Lord, " but they will not enter into the kingdom of heaven because they did not do the will of God. They were not sanctified and perfected in love.

False teachers can never lead a congregation to be holy and righteous. They cannot teach righteousness because they are blind to righteousness. They will not consistently or seriously preach the judgment of God, nor will they seriously and consistently preach against sin because it would offend the flesh and they could not receive glory from men. This would also cause them to lose rewards and numbers which their hearts really love and need to build their fleshly reputation. The powers of darkness are always reminding them of this; they are compromisers of the Word of God. Their hearts are stubborn and hardened. They lead their congregations to resist the Word of God so that their hearts also become hardened. They are at ease in Zion, building *ungodly numbers for God.* These numbers become just like their false teachers: "A blind man cannot guide a blind man, can he? Will they not both fall into a pit? A pupil is not above his teacher; but everyone, after he has been *fully trained, will be like his teacher"* (Luke 6:39, 40).

The powers of darkness deceive the heart of the false teacher by making him believe he needs to look good in order to bring the congregation to God. This is the boastful pride of life. He begins to believe that everything that is good for him — his name and his reputation — is good for God.

He believes that his apparent success has come as a result of God's favor and blessing on him. He is totally bereft of the spiritual understanding and discernment that would show him that the powers of darkness always cooperate with the ones who practice pride and greed. He does not know that both he and his congregation are "... *wretched and miserable and poor and blind and naked"* (Rev. 3:17).

Satan tempted Jesus with the boastful pride of life: "And he (Satan) led Him to Jerusalem and had Him stand on the pinnacle of the temple, and said to Him, 'If You are the Son of God, throw Yourself down from here; for it is written, 'He will give His angels charge concerning You to guard You,' and, 'On their hands they will bear You up, lest You strike Your foot against a stone' " (Luke 4:9-11).

Satan tempted Jesus to seek the approval of men with the boastful pride of life by throwing himself down from the pinnacle of the temple. The angels would save Him and then Jesus would look good to the people in the flesh. This was Satan's way to get Jesus to lead the people with his fleshly reputation.

If Jesus had chosen to lead the people with a fleshly reputation, then Satan knew he could block Jesus from being led by the Spirit of God. He would have captured Jesus in the boastful pride of life — *doing works FOR God instead of God working through Him.*

The boastful pride of life tries to lead people to God without being led by the Spirit of God. This is done through the works of the flesh, using carnal doctrines and carnal traditions. Satan knows that a leader who loves the boastful pride of life will not lead a congregation to deny themselves or take up their cross because he needs to look good after the flesh to his congregation.

Therefore, the congregation is led after the flesh. The real sin in the boastful pride of life is seeking the approval of men rather than the approval of God.

Jesus said: "How can you believe, when you receive glory (approval) from one another, and you do not seek the glory (approval) that is from the one and only God?" (John 5:44). "... Many even of the rulers believed in Him, but because (they wanted the approval) of the Pharisees (their religious leaders) they were not confessing Him, lest they should be put out of the synagogue (church); for they loved the approval of men rather than the approval of God" (John 12:42, 43).

The Psalmist said: *"The boastful shall not stand before Thine eyes;* Thou dost hate all who do iniquity. Thou dost destroy those who speak falsehood (carnal traditions); the Lord abhors the man of bloodshed (who perverts the Word of God) and deceit. There is nothing reliable in what they say; their inward part (heart) is destruction itself; their throat is an open grave (words of death); they flatter with their tongue. Hold them guilty, O God; by their own devices let them fall! In the multitude of their transgressions thrust them out, for they are *rebellious* against Thee" (Ps. 5:5, 6, 9, 10).

When a false teacher is lifted up in pride, the boastful pride of life, *his desire is to look good to the congregation, rather than to God.* He will pick out the blessings in the Bible so he can have the approval of man to fulfill his fleshly ambition. His motive is the boastful pride of life rather than building up the body in unity and to the fullness of Christ. He is a flesh ruler and king. His congregation has appointed a leader to take them back to the slavery of Egypt (the world). They are following another Jesus. Sheep are supposed to recognize the voice (fruit) of false teachers. Their mouths bear the fruit of what is in their hearts. He looked "... like a lamb, and he spoke as a dragon" (Rev. 13:11).

Ezekiel warned: "... Woe, shepherds of Israel who have been feeding themselves! Should not the shepherds feed the flock? 'Is it too slight a thing for you that you should feed in the good pasture (the whole counsel of God's Word), that you must tread down with your feet the rest of your pastures (the other parts of God's Word)? Or that you should drink of the clear waters (the good Word of God), that you must foul (by trampling) the rest (of the gospel) with your feet'? ...

with force and with severity you have *dominated* them (becoming lord over God's heritage)" (Ezek. 34:2, 18, 4).

In other words, after the shepherd reads the whole counsel of God's Word, he picks out the part that will serve his fleshly motives to dominate them and be their king: "And they (the congregation) were scattered (became worldly) for lack of a shepherd, and they became food for every beast of the field (the powers of darkness) and were scattered" (Ezek. 34:5).

The congregations know they are empty but they don't know what will fill the emptiness. They cannot see, hear, or understand the Word of God. They believe they are experiencing the normal Christian life in their shallowness and carnality as they become more and more hardened to the Word of God.

Jesus promised that you would be hated and rejected by the world and the religious leaders when you try to live godly and teach the whole counsel of God's Word. Those who love the flesh nature will oppose those who choose to live holy and godly lives. This is why Jesus said: "Blessed are you when men hate you, and *ostracize you, and cast insults at you, and spurn your name as evil,* for the sake of the Son of Man. Be glad ... for in the same way their fathers used to treat the (true) prophets" (Luke 6:22, 23).

To false preachers and teachers who seek the approval of man to build a name and reputation, rather than preach all of God's Word, Jesus said: "Woe to you *when all men speak well of you* (fleshly approval), for in the same way their fathers used to treat the *false prophets*" (Luke 6:26).

Because a false teacher is deceived, he in turn deceives the congregation: "... Evil men and impostors will proceed from bad to worse, deceiving and being deceived ... for men will be lovers of self, lovers of money, boastful ... holding to a form of godliness ... avoid such men as these" (II Tim. 3:13, 2, 5).

Paul described the situation like this: "Being filled with all (fruit of) unrighteousness, wickedness, greed, evil, full of envy, murder, strife, deceit, malice; they are gossips, slanderers, haters of God, insolent, arrogant, boastful, inventors of evil, disobedient to parents, without understanding, untrustworthy, unloving, unmerciful ..." (Rom. 1:29-31).

He added: "And, although they (false teachers) know the ordinance of God, that those who practice such things (as greed, envy, strife, gossip, slander, arrogance, boasting) are worthy of death, they not only do the same, but also give hearty approval to those who practice them" (Rom. 1:32).

Then, Paul said: "And we know that the *judgment of God rightly falls upon those who practice such things*. But because of your stubborn and unrepentant heart you are stor - ing up *wrath* for yourself in the day of wrath and revelation of the righteous judgment of God, *WHO WILL RENDER TO EVERY MAN ACCORDING TO HIS DEEDS:* to those who by perseverance in doing good ... eternal life; but to those who are *selfishly ambitious* and do not obey the truth ... *wrath and indignation*" (Rom. 2:2, 5-8).

The Psalmist wrote: "God takes a stand in His own congregation; He judges in the midst of the rulers. How long will you judge unjustly, and show partiality to the wicked? Vindicate the weak (who are in bondage) and fatherless (lost); do justice to the afflicted and destitute. Rescue the weak and needy (sick); deliver them out of the hand of the wicked. They do not know nor do they understand; they walk about in darkness" (Ps. 82:1-5).

We are warned: "If anyone advocates a different doctrine, and does not agree with the sound words, those of our Lord Jesus Christ, and with the doctrine (gospel) conforming to godliness (the image of Jesus), he is conceited (pride) and understands nothing (blind teachers); but he has a morbid interest in controversial questions and disputes about words (opposes the truth), out of which arise envy, strife, abusive language, evil suspicions, and constant friction (opposition) between men of depraved mind and deprived of the truth, who suppose that godliness is a means of gain (making the things of God an opportunity for the flesh — name, reputation, pride, greed, rewards)" (I Tim. 6:3-5).

Like the Pharisees, these men attack the gospel with controversial questions in the same way they did the Lord and His disciples. Neither the gospel nor the flesh has changed. They will either repent or attack because the gospel exposes their fleshly kingdoms and carnal traditions which have their hearts. They seek to discredit the messenger who brings the truth so that the truth will not be able to tear down the doctrines and idols which have captured their deceived hearts. If they can make the messenger the object of controversy, it will cause others to take their focus off the message of the Word of God just as the Pharisees did with Jesus.

They will attack the messenger and the truth with controversial statements, such as: "I am afraid he is teaching legalism"; "He is teaching works"; "He doesn't understand grace"; "He will put you under the law"; "He believes Christians can have demons"; "He sees a demon behind every bush"; "He believes Christians can be possessed"; "He believes in sinless perfection"; "He believes all sickness is sin"; or "He does not believe in 'once saved, always saved' "; etc.

Controversial questions draw attention from the real issue: the message of the Word of God. Controversial questions raise suspicions and take the focus off the whitewashed messages of "peace and safety." These controversial questions scare congregations to death and cause them to reject truth without hearing it or examining it.

The result is they hate the one bringing the message without hearing him or the message. The false teacher controls his congregation by making it fearful of hearing the Word from other sources. They also intimidate and withdraw fellowship from those who get a drink of water through someone else. The congregation learns to "hear" God only through their flesh kings.

Since false teachers love pride, they are very jealous of numbers which fulfill their selfish ambition. They will oppose the Word of God and persecute the messengers in order to draw numbers to their fleshly ambition.

An example of this is in the book of Acts: "Paul and Barnabas were preaching on the Sabbath in Antioch, and ... nearly the whole city assembled to hear the word of God. But *when the Jews (the religious leaders) saw the crowds (numbers) they were FILLED WITH JEALOUSY,* and began *CONTRADICTING* the things (Word of God) spoken by Paul and were blaspheming. And Paul and Barnabas spoke out boldly and said, 'It was necessary that the word of God should be spoken to you first; since you *REPUDIATE (AND CONTRADICT) IT* (the Word of God) and *JUDGE YOURSELVES UNWORTHY OF ETERNAL LIFE* ..." (Acts 13:44-46).

This is how Satan uses pride, greed, selfish ambition, and jealousy to oppose and block the Word of God. Those who love selfish ambition are tools of the powers of darkness.

In the Acts of the Apostles we read: "And the word of the Lord was being spread through the whole region. But the Jews (religious leaders) aroused the *devout women of prominence* (who had a fleshly reputation) and the *leading men* (who also had a fleshly reputation) ... and *instigated a persecution* against Paul and Barnabas and *drove them out of their district*" (Acts 13:49-50).

Since congregations are trained like the world to honor men and follow men, Satan can easily use men and women who love fleshly reputations to lead congregations to persecute the work of God.

Fleshly congregations are so programmed to follow men they will not move to the light of God's Word without seeing their devout women of prominence and leading men first go to this light. They cannot be led by the Spirit of God in the Word of God because they are led by men. They do not know that they will be waiting forever before an important person who loves selfish ambition will come to the light, unless he first repents. This is a perfect example of how the blind lead the blind to the pit.

Blind teachers lead the blind into a form of godliness. A form of godliness always teaches you that you can practice sin. An example of this would be the distortion of the first letter Paul wrote to the Corinthians, some of whom were still walking after the flesh. They were saying such things as: "... I am of Paul, ... I am of Apollos" (I Cor. 6:9).

Paul was trying to tell them to be mature and overcome the sins they were practicing: "But a natural (fleshly) man does not accept the things of the Spirit of God; for they are foolishness to him, and he cannot understand them, because they are spiritually appraised" (I Cor. 2:14).

Paul said: "And I brethren, could not speak to you as spiritual men, but as to men of flesh, as to babes in Christ" (I Cor. 3:1).

We all began as babes in Christ but we overcome and put to death the deeds of the flesh. Paul said: "I gave you milk to drink, not solid food ... for you are still fleshly. For since there is jealousy and strife among you, are you not walking like mere men (men of the world)?" (I Cor. 3:2, 3).

When these particular scriptures are used to justify practicing sin, a person has tunnel vision. He will not examine the truth in other parts of the Bible which plainly teach you that you may not continue to practice sin.

People will say today: "It is okay to practice sin because babes in Christ practice strife and jealousy." Do not have tunnel vision like others. Let's look at the rest of the Bible.

Remember that strife and jealousy are the works of the flesh: "For if you are living according to the flesh, you must die; but if by the Spirit you are putting to death the deeds of the body (flesh), you will live. For all who are *being led by the Spirit of God, these are sons of God*" (Rom. 8:13, 14).

Paul also said: "But I say, *walk by the Spirit, and you will not carry out the desire of the flesh.* For the flesh sets its desire against the Spirit, and the Spirit against the flesh;

for these are in opposition to one another, so that *you may not do the things that you please* (after the *flesh*). Now the deeds of the flesh are evident, which are: immorality, impurity, sensuality … *STRIFE, JEALOUSY* … and things like these, of which I forewarn you just as I have forewarned you that those who *practice* such things (as strife and jealousy) shall not inherit the kingdom of God" (Gal. 5:16, 17, 19-21).

Very plainly, people who practice strife and jealousy do not inherit the kingdom of God.

Let's look at the second letter Paul wrote to the Corinthians. Paul said: "Here for this third time I am ready to come to you …" (II Cor. 12:14). "For I am afraid (Paul fears for them) that perhaps when I come I may find you to be not what I wish and may be found by you to be not what you wish; *that perhaps there (still) may be strife, jealousy* … I am afraid that when I come again my God may humiliate me before you, and I may mourn (brokenhearted) over many of those who have *sinned in the past (strife and jealousy) and not repented* of the impurity, immorality, and sensuality which they have *practiced*" (II Cor. 12:20-21).

Paul plainly said that he feared that when he returned again they would still be practicing strife and jealousy and would not have repented.

Let me emphasize that Paul was saying: "I am afraid I may find you to be not what I wish (still practicing sin), in which case I'll be found by you not to be what you wish" (because Paul would not distort the gospel to please men. He would point out this fleshly rebellion).

Paul also said: "… Let us therefore lay aside deeds of darkness (flesh) and put on the armor of light … *not in strife and jealousy*. But put on the Lord Jesus Christ, and *make no provision for the flesh* (strife, jealousy) in regard to its lusts" (Rom. 13:12-14).

Paul added: "Test yourselves to see if you are in the faith; examine yourselves! Or do you not recognize this about yourselves, that Jesus Christ is in you — unless indeed you fail the test?" (II Cor. 13:5).

In Romans he wrote: "For the mind set on the flesh is death, but the mind set on the Spirit is life and peace; however, you are not in the flesh but in the Spirit, if indeed the Spirit of God dwells in you" (Rom. 8:6, 9).

If the Spirit of God is in you, you will be led by the Spirit of God to put to death the deeds of the flesh. Otherwise, you are walking in the flesh.

Is it now obvious that men who love the flesh are blind to this part of the Word of God? They develop doctrines that please men and do not conform them to godliness. They do not deal with the parts of the Bible about judgment, holiness, righteousness, resisting the devil, resisting the flesh, resisting the world, church discipline, overcoming, suffering in the flesh, discernment, doctrines of demons, demons, harlotry, and the weapons of warfare against an enemy who came to steal, kill, and destroy you.

We are clearly warned about the false teachers who will pervert the way of truth. Because of their love for greed, they will exploit you with false words: "For this you know with certainty, that no immoral or impure person (the opposite of a pure heart) or covetous man, who is an idolater (who will not give up sin), has an inheritance in the kingdom of Christ and God. Let no one deceive you with empty words, for because of these things the wrath of God comes upon the sons of disobedience (those who continue to practice sin). *Therefore do not be partakers with them*" (Eph. 5:5-7).

Hear the words of Ezekiel: "... You are a land that is not cleansed (washed with the Word) or rained on (Holy Spirit) in the day of indignation (the judgment today). *There is a conspiracy of her prophets in her midst* (they are all saying the same thing, protecting their carnal doctrines and traditions), like a roaring lion tearing the prey. They have devoured lives (taken congregations captive with a form of godliness); they have taken treasure and precious things (the Lord's glory, the Lord's people); they have made many widows in the midst of her. Her priests have done violence to My law (by not teaching obedience and the judgment of the law) and have profaned My holy things; they have made no distinction between the holy and the profane, and they have not taught the difference between the unclean (flesh) and the clean (Spirit); and they hide their eyes from My sabbaths (by failing to enter into peace and rest from their own works), and I am profaned among them (they want people to think I look like them)" (Ezek. 22:24-26).

Ezekiel added: "Her princes (leaders) within her are like wolves tearing the prey, by shedding blood (perverting the Word and leading congregations into lawlessness) and *destroying lives* in order to get dishonest gain (making godliness a means of gain for selfish ambition). And her prophets have smeared whitewash (cover up) for them, seeing false visions and divining lies (traditions and doctrines of men) for them, saying, 'Thus says the Lord God,' when the Lord has not spoken' " (Ezek. 22:27, 28).

"The people of the land have practiced oppression (opposing spiritual things) and committed robbery (exploiting people), and they have wronged the poor (lost) and needy (sick and afflicted) and have oppressed the sojourner without justice. And I searched for a man among them who should build up the wall (hedge) and stand in the gap before Me for the land, that I should not destroy it; but I found no one. Thus I have poured out My indignation (by lowering the hedge) on them; I have consumed them with the *fire of My wrath;* their way I have brought upon their heads,' declares the Lord God" (Ezek. 22:29-31).

The Psalmist wrote: "O Lord, God of vengeance; God of vengeance, shine forth! Rise up, O judge of the earth; render recompense to the proud. How long shall the wicked, O Lord, how long shall the wicked exult? They pour forth words, they speak arrogantly; all who do wickedness vaunt (honor) themselves. They crush Thy people, O Lord, and afflict Thy heritage. They slay the widow and the stranger, and murder the orphans. And they have said, 'The Lord does not see, nor does the God of Jacob pay heed.' Pay heed, you senseless among the people; and when will you understand, stupid ones?" (Ps. 94:1-8).

The Psalmist also said: *"Can a throne of destruction* (who counsels flesh rebellion) *be allied with Thee,* one which devised mischief (rebellion) by decree? They band themselves together (around carnal doctrines) against the life of the *righteous,* and condemn the *innocent* to death. Who will stand up for me against evildoers? Who will take his stand for me against those who do wickedness? But the Lord has been my stronghold, and my God the rock of my refuge. And He has brought back their wickedness upon them, and *will destroy* them in their evil; the Lord our God will destroy them" (Ps. 94:20, 21, 16, 22, 23).

Micah warned: "Thus says the Lord concerning the *PROPHETS WHO LED MY PEOPLE ASTRAY;* when they have something to bite with their teeth (gold, money), they cry, 'PEACE' (no judgment); but against him who puts nothing (no money) in their mouths, they declare holy war. Therefore, it will be night (spiritual darkness) for you — without vision (no revelation), and darkness for you — without divination (no understanding) ... The day will become dark over them. The seers will be ashamed and the diviners will be embarrassed. Indeed, they will all cover their mouths because there is no answer from God" (Micah 3:5-7).

Micah added: "On the other hand I am filled with power — with the Spirit of the Lord — and with justice and courage *TO MAKE KNOWN TO JACOB HIS REBELLIOUS ACT, EVEN TO ISRAEL HIS SIN.* Now hear this, heads (leaders) of the house of Jacob (church) and rulers of the house of Israel, who abhor justice and twist everything that is straight, who build Zion with bloodshed (by leading congregations in lawlessness) and Jerusalem with violent injustice ... Her priests instruct for a price, and her prophets divine for money. Yet they lean on the Lord saying, 'Is not the Lord in our midst? *CALAMITY* (judgment) *will not come upon us*' " (Micah 3:8-11).

Amos said: "Thus says the Lord, 'For three transgressions of Judah and for four I will not revoke its punishment, because they *rejected the law of the Lord* and have not kept His statutes; their lies also have led them astray, those after which their fathers walked (carnal doctrines). So I will send *fire* (the powers of darkness) upon Judah, and it will consume the citadels of Jerusalem.' Thus says the Lord, 'For three transgressions of Israel and for four I will not revoke its punishment, because *THEY SELL THE RIGHTEOUS FOR MONEY* (greed) and the needy (sick and afflicted) for a pair of sandals. And on garments taken as *pledges* they stretch out beside every altar, and in the house of their God they drink the wine (teaching) of those who have been fined (in prison)' " (Amos 2:4-6, 8).

Amos also said: "Woe to those who are at ease in Zion, and to those who feel secure in the mountain of Samaria, the *DISTINGUISHED men* (leaders and rulers) of the foremost of the nations, *TO WHOM THE HOUSE OF ISRAEL* (church) *COMES,* who drink wine from sacrificial bowls while they anoint themselves with the finest of oils, *YET THEY HAVE NOT GRIEVED OVER THE RUIN OF JOSEPH* (the church)" (Amos 6:1, 6).

The powers of darkness have prevailed over the church today. Satan has used false teachers and carnal doctrines to lead congregations into a form of godliness. He has put them to sleep and captured their hearts with a false security by telling them: "You surely shall not die."

The congregations become justified by the words of men rather than the Word of God: "But the Spirit explicitly says that in later times (the last days) some will *fall away from the faith,* paying attention to deceitful spirits and *doctrines of demons*" (I Tim. 4:1).

Satan's doctrine has been the same: to lead people into rebellion against God! "Therefore be careful how you walk, not as unwise men (foolish), but as wise. So then do not be foolish, but understand what the will of the Lord is" (Eph. 5:15, 17). "... This is the will of God, your sanctification (a pure heart) ..." (I Thess. 4:3). "That He (Jesus) might present to Himself the church in all her glory, having no spot or wrinkle or any such thing; but that she should be holy and blameless, that He might sanctify her, having cleansed her (purified their hearts) by the washing of water with the word" (Eph 5:27, 26).

False teachers who walk after selfish ambition love pride. You will know false teachers by their fruits:

• Pride wants to be the center instead of Jesus.

• Pride pleases flesh so it can receive honor and glory from men.

• Pride holds up its own image instead of the image of Christ.

The Bible has given us examples of the selfish ambition of false teachers and their congregations who love pride. You will see these same fleshly congregations today with their false teachers!

• They (pride) establish their own righteousness and do not submit to the righteousness of God (Rom. 10:3).

• They (pride) trusted in themselves that they were righteous and viewed others with contempt (Luke 18:9).

• They (pride) do all their deeds to be noticed by men (approval of men) (Matt. 23:5).

• They (pride) love the places of honor at banquets, and chief seats in the synagogues (Matt. 23:6).

• They (pride) love the respectful greetings in the marketplace and being called by men "Rabbi" (Matt. 23:7).

• They (pride) outwardly (in the flesh) appear righteous to men, but inwardly (in their hearts) are full of hypocrisy and lawlessness (Matt. 23:28).

• They (pride) travel about on sea and land to make a proselyte and he becomes twice as much the son of hell as they are (Matt. 23:15).

• They (pride) tithe, but neglect justice, mercy, and faithfulness (Matt. 23:23).

• They (pride) are blind guides (false teachers), who clean the outside of the cup (to make the flesh look good), but the inside (the heart) is full of robbery and self-indulgence.

• They (pride) are whitewashed tombs which appear beautiful on the outside but inside are full of dead men's bones and all uncleanness (Matt. 23:24-27).

• They (pride) shut off the kingdom of heaven from men for they do not go in themselves nor do they allow those who are entering to go in. Jesus said: "You serpents! You brood of vipers (family of the devil)! *HOW SHALL YOU ESCAPE THE SENTENCE OF HELL?*" (Matt. 23:13, 33).

These leaders always please the flesh and receive their glory from men: "Those who desire to make a *good showing in the flesh* try to compel you to be circumcised (be like them), simply that they may not be persecuted for the cross of Christ. For those who are circumcised do not even keep the law themselves, but they desire to have you circumcised (in bondage to their works), *that they may boast in your flesh*" (Gal. 6:12, 13). *"They eagerly seek you,* not commendably (wrong motives), but they wish to shut you out *in order that you may seek them"* (Gal. 4:17).

These false teachers seek you with fleshly motives (not commendably) in order that you may seek them and they may become your king. They then use you in their fleshly manipulation and schemes to help them seek others to enlarge their fleshly kingdom.

Hear again the words of Ezekiel: "Son of man, prophesy against the prophets of Israel who prophesy, and say to those who prophesy (preach) from their own inspiration, 'Listen to the word of the Lord!' Thus says the Lord God, 'Woe to the foolish prophets who are *following their own spirit* and have seen nothing' ... *You have not gone up into the breaches* (to resist the powers of darkness), nor did you *build the wall* (hedge) around the house of Israel to stand in the battle on the day of the Lord. They see *falsehood* (carnal doctrines) and *lying divination* (false dreams) who are saying, 'The Lord declares,' when the Lord has not sent them; yet *they hope for the fulfillment of their word* (so they can build their self-image)" (Ezek. 13:2, 3, 5, 6).

Ezekiel also pointed out: " 'Did you not see a false vision and speak a lying divination when you said, 'The Lord declares,' 'but it is not I who have spoken.' 'Therefore,' thus says the Lord God, 'Because you have spoken falsehood and seen a lie, therefore behold, *I am against you,*' declares the Lord God. 'So My hand will be against the prophets who see false visions and utter lying divination. They will have *no place* in the council of My people, nor will they be written down in the register of the house of Israel ..." (Ezek. 13:7-9).

Ezekiel also said: "It is definitely because they have *misled My people* by saying, 'Peace!' when there is no peace. (The prophets tell the people, 'It's alright to walk in sin; no judgment will come upon you!') And when anyone builds a wall, behold, they plaster it over with whitewash (this whitewashed wall is a false hedge of protection); so tell those who plaster it over with whitewash (cover up), that it will fall. A flooding rain will come (the powers of darkness against the foundations), and you, O hailstones, will fall ... thus I shall spend *My wrath on the wall (false hedge) and on those who have plastered it over with whitewash;* and I shall say to you, 'The wall (false hedge) is gone and its plasterers are gone, along with the prophets of Israel who prophesy to Jerusalem, and who see visions of peace for her when there is no peace (no hedge of protection),' declares the Lord God" (Ezek. 13:10, 11, 15, 16).

Jeremiah wrote: " 'I have heard what the prophets have said who prophesy falsely in My name, saying, 'I had a dream, I had a dream!' How long? Is there anything in the hearts of the prophets who prophesy falsehood, even these prophets of the deception of their own heart, who intend to *make My people forget My name by their dreams* which they relate to one another, just as their fathers forgot My name because of Baal (idols)? The prophet who has a dream may relate his dream, but let him who has My word speak My word in truth. What does straw (stubble) have in common with grain (fruit)?' declares the Lord" (Jer. 23:25-28).

Isaiah wrote: "Listen to Me, you who pursue righteousness, who seek the Lord. Look to the *rock* (Jesus) from which you were hewn" *"DO NOT FEAR THE REPROACH OF MAN,* neither be dismayed at their revilings (persecution)" (Isa. 51:1, 7).

Paul wrote to the Thessalonians: "Now we request you, brethren, with regard to the coming of our Lord Jesus Christ, and our gathering together to Him ... Let no one in any way deceive you, for it will not come unless the apostasy (falling away from the faith) comes first ... and then that lawless one will be revealed ... that is, the one whose coming is in accord with the *activity of Satan,* with *all power* and *signs* and *false wonders,* and with all the *deception of wickedness* for those who perish, because they *did not receive the love of the truth so as to be saved.* (Their hearts went after signs and wonders rather than God's Word.). And for this reason God will send upon them a deluding influence (religious spirits) so that they might believe what is false ..." (II Thess. 2:1, 3, 8-11).

God warned Adam if he ate of the tree of (death or) the knowledge of good and evil (lust of the flesh, lust of the eyes, and the boastful pride of life): "... you shall surely die" (Gen. 2:17). Satan then tempted and enticed Eve to eat from the tree of death, by saying: "... *YOU SURELY SHALL NOT DIE!"* (Gen. 3:4).

This is a direct contradiction of the Word of God and is the first reference to a doctrine of Satan in the Bible. Eve was led astray by a different spirit, another doctrine, and another gospel: "Then the Lord God said to the woman,

'What is this you have done?' And the woman said, 'The serpent deceived me and I ate' " (Gen. 3:13).

When we receive the teaching of false teachers, their words become the fruit of death and lead us to rebel against God. Satan is still leading people to the tree of sin and death today to eat the fruit of the knowledge of good and evil. This tree of death is false teaching which does not warn people about sin. Satan uses false teachers to give congregations a false security by telling them: "... YOU SURELY SHALL NOT DIE' " (Gen. 3:4). If a false watchman does not warn his congregation about breaking God's laws by sinning, the congregation then has no protection from God. They are destroyed in their iniquity because of the false words of a false watchman who told them "YOU SURELY SHALL NOT DIE." He led his congregation to destruction while he fulfilled his own selfish ambition.

We see a clear warning to the false watchman and his congregation in Ezekiel: " ' ... If the watchman sees the sword (curse) coming and *does not blow the trumpet, and the people are not warned,* and a sword (curse) comes and takes a person from them, he is taken away in his iniquity; but his blood I will require from the watchman's hand.' When I say to the wicked, 'O wicked man, YOU SHALL SURELY DIE,' and you do not speak to *warn the wicked* from his way (sin), that wicked man shall die in his iniquity, but his blood I will require from your hand. (A false watchman sheds the blood of his congregation by leading them to destruction.) But if you on your part warn a wicked man to turn from his way (*or you surely shall die*) and he does not turn from his way (sin), he will die in his iniquity; but you have delivered your life' " (Ezek. 33:6, 8, 9).

Ezekiel also wrote: " 'Now as for you, son of man, say to the house of Israel, 'Thus you have spoken, saying, surely our transgressions and our sins are upon us, and we are rotting away in them; (in sickness and destruction). (This is God's judgment on a fallen-away church today); how then can we survive?' SAY TO THEM, 'As I live!' declares the

Lord God, 'I take no pleasure in the death of the wicked, but rather that the wicked turn from his way (breaking God's laws) and live. TURN BACK, TURN BACK, FROM YOUR EVIL WAYS! WHY THEN WILL YOU DIE, O HOUSE OF ISRAEL?' " (Ezek. 33:10, 11).

The gospel from God through our Lord Jesus Christ says: *"You shall surely die"* if you practice sin. False teachers, controlled by pride and greed and Satan, are flattering and exploiting congregations while they lead them into sin and destruction.

Jude warns about these false teachers, they: "... turn the grace of our God into licentiousness (a license to sin) and deny our only Master and Lord, Jesus Christ. Now I desire to remind you ... that the Lord after saving a people out of the land of Egypt, subsequently *destroyed* those who did not believe (sinned)" (Jude 4, 5).

Satan's kings of pride and greed are *real nice fellows* who lead people from the faith into destruction while they use parts of God's Word, God's people, carnal doctrines and ungodly traditions, to fulfill their selfish love for the nature of Satan. Paul said: "And no wonder, for even Satan disguises himself as an angel of light. Therefore it is not surprising if his servants also disguise themselves as servants of righteousness; whose end shall be according to their deeds" (II Cor. 11:14, 15).

Paul wrote to the Corinthians: *"But I am afraid, lest as the serpent deceived Eve by his craftiness, your minds should be led astray from the simplicity and purity (a pure heart) of devotion to Christ. For if one comes and PREACHES ANOTHER JESUS whom we have not preached, or you receive a DIFFERENT SPIRIT which you have not received, or a DIFFERENT GOSPEL which you have not accepted, you bear this beautifully. For you bear with anyone if he enslaves you, if he devours you, if he takes advantage of you, if he exalts himself ... For I am jealous for you (your hearts) with a godly jealousy; for I betrothed you to one husband, that to

Christ I might present you as a PURE VIRGIN *(pure heart)"*
(II Cor. 11:3, 4, 20, 2).

True prophets and teachers will build up the body of
Christ "... until we all attain to the unity of the faith ... to
a mature man (a pure heart) ... to the fulness of Christ. As a
result, we are no longer ... carried about by *EVERY WIND
OF DOCTRINE, BY THE TRICKERY OF MEN (who love
selfish ambition), BY CRAFTINESS IN DECEITFUL
SCHEMING* (to build earthly and fleshly kingdoms)"
(Eph. 4:13, 14).

8

Hear the Word of the Lord, You Rulers of Sodom

The following scriptures are serious warnings to the fleshly rulers today: " *'Hear the word of the Lord, you rulers of Sodom* (flesh kings); Give ear to the instructions of our God, you people (congregation) of Gomorrah (who walk after the flesh)' " (Isa. 1:10). " 'Woe to the shepherds who are destroying and scattering the sheep of My pasture!' declares the Lord ... 'You have scattered My flock and driven them away, and have not attended to them; behold, I am about to attend to you ...' " (Jer. 23:1, 2).

" 'I have heard what the prophets have said who prophesy (preach) falsely in My name, saying, 'I had a dream, I had a dream!' ... even these prophets of the deception of their own heart, who intend to make My people forget My name by their dreams (of fleshly achievements) which they relate to one another ... For you will no longer remember the oracle (Word) of the Lord, because every man's own word will become the oracle, and you have perverted the words of the living God ...' " (Jer. 23:25-27).

"How the faithful city (church) has become a harlot, she who was full of justice! Righteousness once lodged in her, but now murderers. Your silver has become dross, your drink (the Word of God) diluted with water (watered down).

Your rulers (leaders) are rebels, and companions of thieves; everyone loves a bribe, and chases after rewards (greed) ..." (Isa. 1:21, 23).

"Surely, you will be ashamed of the oaks (strong men after the flesh) which you have desired, and you will be embarrassed at the gardens which you have chosen. And the strong man will become tinder (dried up), his work also a spark (wood, hay, and stubble), thus they shall both burn together ..." (Isa. 1:29, 31).

"Their land has also been filled with idols; they worship the work of their hands ... For the Lord of hosts will have a day of reckoning against everyone who is lifted up ... And the pride of man will be humbled, and the loftiness of men will be abased, and the Lord alone will be exalted in that day" (Isa. 2:8, 12, 17). "Stop *regarding man,* whose breath of life is in his nostrils; for why should he be esteemed? O my people! ... *Those who guide you lead you astray,* and confuse the direction of your path" (Isa. 2:22; 3:12).

" 'Also among the prophets (preachers) of Jerusalem (church), I have seen a horrible thing; the committing of adultery and walking in falsehood (carnal doctrines); and they strengthen the hands of (fleshly) evildoers, so that *NO ONE HAS TURNED BACK FROM HIS WICKEDNESS* (flesh). All of them have become to Me like Sodom and her inhabitants like Gomorrah' " (Jer. 23:14).

" 'They keep saying to those (their congregations) who despise Me (by loving the flesh), the Lord has said, 'You will have peace' and as for everyone who walks in the stubbornness (rebellion) of his own heart, they say, 'Calamity (judgment) will not come on you!' " (Jer. 23:17). " 'But if they had stood in My council, then they would have announced (all) My words to My people, and would have *turned them back* from their evil way and from the evil of their deeds (lusts)' " (Jer. 23:22).

" ' ... Go and tell this people, (you) keep on listening but do not perceive; (you) keep on looking, but do not understand" (Isa. 6:9). " 'For those who guide this people are leading them astray; and those who are guided by them are brought to confusion' " (Isa. 9:16). "They have dealt treacherously against the Lord, for they have borne illegitimate children" (Hosea 5:7). " 'Woe to those who enact evil statutes, and to those who constantly record unjust decisions' " (Isa. 10:1).

"Now what will you do in the day of punishment, and in the devastation which will come from afar? To whom will you flee for help? And where will you leave your wealth?" (Isa. 10:3). "For from the least of them even to the greatest of them, everyone is greedy for gain, and from the prophet even to the priest, everyone deals falsely (selfish motives)' " (Jer. 6:13). " 'They have spoken what is not right (traditions of men); no man repented of his wickedness, saying, 'What have I done?' Everyone turned to his course (self centeredness) ..." (Jer. 8:6).

The Lord Is Destroying
The Pastures of the Shepherds

" 'As they had their pasture (their own church), they became satisfied, and being satisfied their heart became proud; therefore, they forgot Me. It is your destruction, O Israel, that you are against Me, against your help' " (Hosea 13:6, 9).

"Thus says the Lord of hosts, 'Behold, evil (the powers of darkness) is going forth from nation to nation, and a great storm is being stirred up from the remotest parts of the earth. Wail, you SHEPHERDS, and cry; and wallow in ashes, you MASTERS OF THE FLOCK (lords over God's heritage); for the days of your slaughter and your dispersions have come, and you shall fall like a choice vessel' " (Jer. 25:32, 34).

"Flight shall perish from the shepherds, and escape from the masters of the flock. Hear the sound of the cry of the shepherds, and the wailing of the masters of the flock! For the Lord is destroying their pasture" (Jer. 25:35, 36).

"There is a sound of the shepherds' wail, for their glory is ruined; there is a sound of the young lions' roar (the powers of darkness), for the pride of the Jordan is ruined. Those who buy them slay them and go unpunished, and each of those who sell them (for a reputation) says, 'Blessed be the Lord, for I have become rich (fleshly achievements)!' And their own shepherds have no pity on them. For I shall no longer have pity on the inhabitants of the land,' declares the Lord; 'but behold, I shall cause the men to fall, each into another's power and into the power of his king (Satan); and they (the powers of darkness) will strike the land (kill, steal, and destroy), and I shall not deliver them from their power' " (Zech. 11:3, 5, 6).

" 'Ephraim (the church) mixes himself with the nations (world); Ephraim has become a cake not turned (harlotry). *STRANGERS* (powers of darkness) *DEVOUR HIS STRENGTH, YET HE DOES NOT KNOW IT* ... Though the pride of Israel testifies against him, yet they have neither repented to the Lord their God, nor have they sought Him, for all this' " (Hosea 7:8-10).

"PUT THE TRUMPET TO YOUR LIPS! *Like an eagle the enemy comes against the house of the Lord,* because they have transgressed My covenant, and *rebelled against My law.* Israel has rejected the good; the enemy will pursue him. They have set up kings (rulers after the flesh), *but not by Me;* they have appointed princes (leaders), but I did not know it. With their silver and gold they have made idols for themselves, that they might be cut off (destroyed). He has rejected your calf, O Samaria, saying, 'My anger burns against them!' How long will they be incapable of innocence?' " (Hosea 8:1, 3-5).

" 'They feed on the sin of My people, and direct their desire toward their iniquity. *And it will be, like people, like priest;* So I will punish them for their ways, and repay them for their deeds' " (Hosea 4:8, 9). " 'Ephraim (the church) is oppressed, crushed in judgment, *because he was determined to follow man's command'* " (Hosea 5:11).

" 'For they sow the wind (words instead of the Word), and they reap the whirlwind (judgment). The standing grain has no heads; it yields no grain (no fruit). Should it yield, strangers (the powers of darkness) would swallow it up. Israel is swallowed up; they are now among the nations (the world) like a vessel in which no one delights. Since Ephraim has multiplied altars for sin (congregations who honor flesh), they have become altars of sinning for him. Though I wrote for him ten thousand precepts of My law, they are regarded as a strange thing' " (Hosea 8:7, 8, 11, 12).

"... Thus He looked for justice, but behold, bloodshed; for righteousness, but behold, a cry of distress (bondage). Therefore My people go into exile (captivity) for their lack of knowledge; and their honorable men are famished, and their multitude is parched with thirst. Therefore Sheol has enlarged its throat and opened its mouth without measure; and Jerusalem's splendor, her multitude, her din of revelry, and the jubilant within her, descend into it (hell)" (Isa. 5:7, 13, 14).

"*Woe to those who call evil good, and good evil;* who substitute darkness for light and light for darkness ... Woe to those who are wise in their own eyes, and clever in their own sight! ... who justify the wicked for a bribe, and take away the rights of the ones who are in the right (the righteous)! ... Their root will become like rot and their blossom blow away as dust (bear no fruit); for *they have rejected the law of the Lord of hosts,* and despised the word of the Holy One (Jesus) of Israel" (Isa. 5:20, 21, 23, 24.)

" 'And they have healed the brokenness of My people superficially, saying 'Peace, Peace,' but there is no peace" (Jer. 6:14).

" 'Israel (the church) is a luxuriant (degenerate) vine; *he produces fruit for himself* (selfish ambition). The more his fruit (of selfish ambition), the more altars (church buildings) he made (expanding fleshly kingdoms); the richer his land, the better he made the sacred pillars (palaces for fleshly kings). Their heart is faithless; now they must bear their guilt. The Lord will break down their altars and destroy their sacred pillars ... You have reaped injustice, *you have eaten the fruit of lies*. Because you have *trusted in your way, in your numerous warriors* (numbers)' " (Hosea 10:1, 2, 13).

" 'The days of punishment have come, the days of retribution have come; Let Israel know this! The prophet is a fool, the inspired man is demented, because of the grossness of your iniquity, and because your hostility (rebellion) is so great!' " (Hosea 9:7). "The Lord has accomplished His wrath, He has poured out His fierce anger; and He has kindled a *fire* in Zion which has consumed its *foundations*. The kings of the earth did not believe, nor did any of the inhabitants of the world, *that the adversary and the enemy (the powers of darkness) could enter the gates of Jerusalem (the church), because of the sins of her prophets and the iniquities of her priests (preachers), who have shed the blood of the righteous (because they perverted the Word)*" (Lam. 4:11-13).

9

Wake Up, Wake Up Sleeping Virgins

We are now living in the time of the most alarming condition that has ever existed in church history. Satan and the powers of darkness are no longer restrained. The hedge is being removed. Never have there been such problems, pressures, divisions, confusion, suspicion, and hate as exist in the church today. This is the shaking of the last days and this is the day of the Lord. The judgment of God has come upon us.

The wise virgins and the foolish virgins alike have fallen asleep. A trumpet of warning is now blowing: "For this reason it says, 'Awake, sleeper, and arise from the dead, and Christ will shine on you.' Therefore, be careful how you walk, not as unwise men (foolish virgins), but as wise (virgins)" (Eph. 5:14, 15).

Jesus Christ is returning at a time of great spiritual darkness (midnight), while everyone is drowsy and sleeping: "Now while the bridegroom was delaying, they all got drowsy and began to sleep. But at *midnight* there was a shout (trumpet blowing), 'Behold, the bridegroom! Come out to meet Him' " (Matt. 25:5, 6). Those who have ears to hear will come out to meet the bridegroom. The others will remain asleep.

At this time of great spiritual darkness, God is giving great revelation in order that the wise virgins can wake up, come out of darkness, and meet the bridegroom. The wise virgins will have spiritual ears to hear the trumpet warning and will wake up. The reason they will have ears to hear and eyes to see is because their trust is in the Lord rather than men and carnal traditions. The foolish virgins will not wake up. Their hearts are trained to receive only messages of peace and safety. Since they have a false security, they will remain asleep and will not listen to the trumpet warning. Since the foolish virgins are not led by the Spirit of God, they have no oil (Spirit) (Matt. 25:4).

John the Apostle wrote in Revelation: "And the dragon was enraged with the woman, and went off to make war with the rest of her offspring, who keep the commandments of God and hold to the testimony of Jesus" (Rev. 12:17).

Satan is bringing increasing trials and tribulations against the church today. Everyone whose foundation is not the Word of God will *react* to these fiery trials and pressures *after the flesh* and commit lawlessness (sin).

This is the reason the powers of darkness will be able to get more and more ground to destroy all those whose foundation is a "form" of godliness. These are the foolish virgins of the false church, Babylon, who will be burned in this fire. However, the wise virgins will stand on the Word of God and die to all fleshly rebellion because of their faith and obedience. They will be protected from the fire by the hedge of God because they do not break God's law.

Everything God does, Satan attempts to counterfeit. For example, God has a river that flows out of His mouth (which is the Word of God) that brings life and peace to all those who will receive it. On the other hand, Satan has a river which flows out of his mouth (which are his suggestions coming as thoughts to our flesh nature). When we receive the words of Satan and act upon them, they cause us to commit lawlessness which brings death. This is how we are carried away and destroyed by the flood of words which come from the mouth of Satan.

God's words bring life and Satan's words bring death: "And *the serpent poured water (words) like a river out of his mouth after the woman (church), so that he might cause her to be swept away with the flood (of words).* And they (the true church) overcame him because of the blood of the Lamb and because of the word of their testimony, and *they did not love their (fleshly) life even to death*" (Rev. 12:15, 11).

These are the wise virgins who act upon the Word of God. Satan could get no ground in their lives with his flood of words (temptations) because they had laid down their lives and no longer loved the flesh.

Jesus said, "... Everyone who hears these words of Mine, and *does not act upon them,* will be like a *foolish man* (foolish virgin), who built his house upon the *sand* (carnal doctrines) ... And the *floods came* (which are the words, trials, and temptations of the powers of darkness) ... and burst against that house; and it fell (carried away), and *great was its fall*" (Matt. 7:26, 27).

Today is the day of the Lord. God's judgment has come upon the worldly church that is practicing lawlessness. We are now living in the beginning of this great destruction as hordes upon hordes of demons have already been unleashed against Babylon, the harlot church today. The One who has restrained them is removing His hedge: "And though they hide on the summit of Carmel, I will search them out and take them from there; and though they conceal themselves from My sight on the floor of the sea, from there I will command the serpent (powers of darkness) and it will bite them" (Amos 9:3).

God is revealing to us now how the powers of darkness (who are the lawless ones) lead us into lawlessness and destruction. This is the reason the powers of darkness who are sons of the devil are called *sons of destruction.* Their whole purpose is to propagate rebellion to God's law so they can kill, steal and destroy. For the day of the Lord "... will not come unless the *apostasy comes first* (this has already happened), and the *man of lawlessness is revealed, the son of destruction* (which are the powers of darkness), *who opposes and exalts himself* above every so-called god or object of worship, so that *HE TAKES HIS SEAT IN THE TEMPLE OF GOD* (which is our bodies), displaying himself as being God (by controlling our hearts and lives)" (II Thess. 2:3, 4).

While a sleeping church waits for a physical temple to be built in Israel, they are blinded to the fact that they are a part of a spiritual falling away. The spiritual is taking place while they are waiting for the physical. The man of lawlessness, the son of destruction, has already led the church into lawlessness and entered their temples. This is how Babylon is a dwelling place of demons. The powers of darkness are the abomination that enters the temple to make desolation in the last days. To have understanding about the mystery of lawlessness is to simply understand how the man of lawlessness (the powers of darkness) tempt and lead mankind in rebellion to God's laws so they can destroy them.

The powers of darkness have used another gospel, another Jesus and doctrines of demons to bring about the apostasy, the great falling away and destruction of the church today: "Oh, God, why hast Thou rejected us forever? *Why does Thine anger smoke against* the sheep of Thy pasture? Remember *THY CONGREGATION,* which Thou hast purchased of old, which Thou hast *redeemed* to be the tribe of *Thine inheritance* ... Turn Thy footsteps toward the perpetual ruins; the *enemy* (the powers of darkness) has damaged everything *within the sanctuary* (our bodies which are the temples of God). *Thine adversaries have (also) roared in the midst of Thy meeting place* (the lions roar because they have captured the meeting places); *they have set up their own standards (doctrines of demons) for signs.* It seems as if one (tree cutter) had lifted up his axe in a forest of trees (cut down the congregation). (The powers of darkness are the tree cutters). *They have BURNED Thy sanctuary to the ground; they have DEFILED the dwelling place of Thy name ... THEY HAVE BURNED ALL THE MEETING PLACES OF GOD IN THE LAND.* We do not see our signs (stumbling and staggering in spiritual darkness); There is no longer any prophet, nor is there any among us who knows how long. How long, O God, will the adversary revile ... ?" (Ps. 74:1-5, 7-10).

The prophet Obadiah said: " 'For the day of the Lord draws near on all the nations. *As you have done, it will be done to you* (blessings or the curses of the law). Your dealings will return on your own head. But on Mt. Zion there will be those (the remnant) who escape, and it will be holy. And the house of Jacob (the church) will possess their possessions ... but the house of Esau (the house of flesh) will be as stubble. And they will set them on fire and consume them, so that there will be no survivor of the house of Esau (flesh),' for the Lord has spoken" (Obad. 1:15, 17, 18).

Isaiah said: "... And the hand of the Lord shall be made known to His servants, and He shall be *INDIGNANT toward His enemies.* For behold, *the Lord will come in fire* ... to render His anger with fury and His rebuke with flames of fire. For the Lord will execute judgment by fire and by His sword (the curse) on all flesh, and those slain by the Lord will be many" (Isa. 66:14-16).

These scriptures describe what the powers of darkness are doing today. This is the day of the Lord: "... For the day of the Lord is near, for the Lord has prepared a sacrifice, *He has consecrated His guests"* (Zeph. 1:7). His guests are the powers of darkness. He is lowering the hedge on a people who hate and reject His Word. The powers of darkness are executing the anger and indignation of God. These tree cutters have taken over the meeting places with doctrines of demons as they destroy the worldly and backslidden congregations. Most of the sleeping church does not even know they are a dwelling place of demons: "... And *it set him aflame* all around, *yet he did not recognize it; and it burned him, BUT HE PAID NO ATTENTION"* (Isa. 42:25).

In the book of Isaiah we read: "I have commanded My consecrated ones (the powers of darkness), I have called *My mighty warriors* (God's army of vengeance and destruction), *My proudly exulting ones, to execute My anger"* (Isa. 13:3).

God's proudly exulting warriors are the army of darkness that God has unleashed against the false church. They execute God's wrath in vengeance for the lawlessness of the church. Just as God sent an evil spirit to Saul for transgressing His command, He is doing the same today (I Sam. 15:22-24; 16:14, 15). Not one demon does anything without the permission of God.

Isaiah also wrote: "A sound of tumult on the mountains ... *the Lord of Hosts is mustering the ARMY FOR BATTLE.* They are coming from a far country from the farthest horizons (end of heaven), the Lord (is coming) *AND HIS INSTRUMENTS OF INDIGNATION, TO DESTROY THE WHOLE LAND"* (Isa. 13:4, 5). This army is already surrounding Jerusalem (the church) today.

Isaiah added: "Wail, for the day of the Lord is near! *It will come as destruction from the Almighty.* And they will be terrified, pains and anguish will take hold of them; *they will writhe like a woman in labor (with birth pangs),* they will look at one another in *astonishment* (because they have been asleep), their *faces aflame.* Behold, the day of the Lord is coming, cruel, with fury and burning anger, to make the land a *desolation* (the powers of darkness are the abomination that makes desolation); and He will exterminate its sinners from it. Thus I will punish the world for its evil, and the wicked for their iniquity. *I will also put an end to the arrogance of the proud, and abase the haughtiness of the ruthless"* (Isa. 13:6, 8, 9, 11).

In the book of Matthew we find: "Therefore just as the tares are gathered up and burned with fire, so shall it be at the end of the age ... the angels shall come forth, and take out the wicked from among the righteous ... they will gather out of His kingdom all *stumbling blocks,* and *those* who *commit lawlessness,* and will cast them into the *furnace of fire;* in that place there shall be weeping and gnashing of teeth. Then the righteous (wise virgins) will shine forth as the sun in the kingdom of their Father. He who has (spiritual) ears, let him hear" (Matt. 13:40, 49, 41-43).

This day is upon us. The trumpet is blowing loudly and clearly. Those who have *wise hearts* will hear this warning. Those with *foolish hearts* will never wake up until it is too late: "So then do not be foolish, but *understand what the will of the Lord is*" (Eph. 5:17). " 'Not everyone who says to Me, "Lord, Lord," ' will enter the kingdom of heaven; but *he who does the will of My Father who is in heaven'* " (Matt. 7:21). The foolish virgins think they are doing the will of God. They don't even know the Lord. Their foundation will not stand in the day of the Lord's destruction.

The writer of Hebrews said: "See to it that you do not refuse Him who is speaking. For if those did not escape when they refused him who warned them on earth, much less shall we escape who turn away from Him who warns from heaven. And His voice shook the earth then, but now He has promised, saying, *'YET ONCE MORE I WILL SHAKE NOT ONLY THE EARTH, BUT ALSO THE HEAVEN'* ... 'Yet once more' denotes the *removing of those things which can be shaken ...* in order that *those things which cannot be shaken may remain*" (Heb. 12:25-27.)

This shaking is the judgment God pronounces in these last days. This judgment is the *shaking of every foundation.* This shaking is the *(spiritual) earthquake* of the last days. Everyone who is standing on a foundation that is not the Word of God will be removed and destroyed in this spiritual earthquake of the last days. The powers of darkness will be able to destroy everyone whose foundation is sand because they are transgressors of the law of God. Only the wise virgins will survive the day of the Lord. They cannot be shaken because their foundation is the Word of God. They will be protected by God and shine forth as the sun.

The Word tells us: "Therefore everyone who hears these words of Mine, and acts upon them, may be compared to a *wise man* (wise virgin), who built his house upon a rock (the Word of God)" (Matt. 7:24). "... And when a flood rose (temptations of the powers of darkness), the torrent (river) burst against that house and *COULD NOT SHAKE IT,* because it had been well built" (Luke 6:48).

Only those (a remnant) who cannot be shaken will survive this destruction. They will act upon the Word of God, not carnal doctrines. The foolish virgins who have the wrong foundation do not obey God's Word. They are asleep and walking in darkness. The trumpet is blowing but they will not receive any warning about judgment. They will only receive messages of "peace and safety" because of their false security. Listen to the words of Matthew: "For the coming of the Son of Man will be just like the days of Noah" (Matt. 24:37).

In those days they were asleep, just as the church is asleep today, and they scoffed about the judgment of God just as they will scoff about the judgment of God today: *"And just as it happened in the days of Noah, so it shall be also in the days of the Son of Man:* they were eating, they were drinking, they were marrying, they were being given in marriage, until the day that Noah entered the ark, and the flood (of water) came and destroyed them all. *IT WILL BE JUST THE SAME* on the day the Son of Man is revealed" (Luke 17:26, 27, 30).

The flood of water brought destruction during the days of Noah. The powers of darkness are bringing the flood of words to destroy today. Since the coming of the Son of Man will bring destruction just as in the days of Noah, we need to see why they were destroyed in the days of Noah: "Then the Lord saw that the wickedness of man was great upon the earth, and that *every intent of the thoughts of his heart was only evil continually* (as it is today). And the Lord was sorry that He had made man on the earth ... and the Lord said, 'I will blot out man whom I have created from the face of the land ... but Noah found favor in the eyes of God ... *Noah was a righteous man, blameless in his time, Noah walked with God"* (Gen. 6:5-9).

Genesis also tells us: "And God looked on the earth, and behold, it was corrupt; for *all flesh had corrupted their way* upon the earth (as they have today). Then God said to Noah, 'The end of all flesh has come before Me ... I am about to destroy them ... I, even I am *bringing the flood of water upon the earth, to destroy all flesh* ... (God is destroying with a spiritual flood today) ... Everything that is on the earth shall *perish.'* " God said, " *'But I will establish My covenant with you* (since Noah was a righteous man, blameless, and walked with God); and *YOU SHALL ENTER THE ARK* ...' " (Gen. 6:12, 13, 17, 18).

We can see that this is also an example and instruction for us today to a sleeping church to wake up and enter the ark: "Then the Lord said to Noah, *'ENTER THE ARK, you and all your household, FOR YOU ALONE I HAVE SEEN TO BE RIGHTEOUS BEFORE ME IN THIS TIME.'* Then Noah ... entered the ark because of the water of the flood, and the rain fell upon the earth for forty days and forty nights. And those that entered, male and female of all flesh, *entered (the ark) as God had commanded him; and the Lord closed it (the door) behind him.* And the water (flood) prevailed more and more upon the earth (as the rain and flood are prevailing today) ... Thus He blotted out every living thing that was upon the face of the land ... and *only Noah was left,* together with those that were with him *IN THE ARK"* (Gen. 7:1, 7, 16, 19, 23).

Everyone else was destroyed. This is what is happening to us today. It is raining now. Matthew gives an account of how the foolish (virgins) will be swept away in this flood of destruction: "And everyone who hears these words of Mine, and *does not act upon them,* will be like a *foolish man* (foolish virgin) who built his house upon *sand* (wrong foundation, carnal doctrines), and the *RAIN DESCENDED,* and the FLOODS (temptations) came, and the winds (storm) blew, and burst against that house (foolish virgins), and it fell, and *great was its fall* "(Matt. 7:26, 27).

It is raining more and more each day. They were asleep in the days of Noah; they are asleep now. The most terrible time that has ever come upon the earth since the beginning of mankind is upon us today.

Just as the flood of waters destroyed the ungodly in the days of Noah, the ungodly will be destroyed by a flood of destruction today. This is the day of the Lord's violence and judgment against a stubborn and obstinate people who refuse to repent and enter the ark which is the Lord Jesus Christ. This judgment of God is upon every person whose foundation is sand. God is raining judgment and the fetters will become stronger and stronger each passing day. It is a day of destruction and wrath from God. We are now waking up from a nightmare.

"If anyone advocates a different doctrine and does not agree with sound words, those of our Lord Jesus Christ, and with the doctrine conforming to godliness, he is conceited and *understands nothing* ..." (I Tim. 6:3, 4).

Congregations who follow after doctrines that do not conform them to godliness remain in darkness without understanding. These are the ones in the fortified cities and high corner towers who are swept away by these hordes of darkness, which is the flood: *"And they did not understand until the flood came and took them all away; SO SHALL THE COMING OF THE SON OF MAN BE"* (Matt. 24:39).

John in Revelation wrote: "... If therefore you will not *wake up,* I will come like a thief, and you will not know at what hour *I will come upon you"* (Rev. 3:3).

Matthew said: "Then there shall be two men in the field; one will be *taken* (by the flood of the powers of darkness), and one will be left. Two women will be grinding at the mill; one will be taken (by the flood), and one will be left. Therefore be on the alert, for you do not know which day your Lord is coming. But be sure of this, that if the head of the house had known at what time of the *night* (spiritual darkness) the thief (powers of darkness) was coming, he would have been on the alert and would not have allowed his house (temple) to be broken into" (Matt. 24:40-43). Only those who have spiritual ears to hear will receive this warning. The others will scoff as they did in the days of Noah.

Revelation 19 tells us about two suppers. One supper described in verses 7-9 is the marriage supper of the Lamb. This is for the *bride* of Christ who has *made herself ready*. She knows the will of God. She is a wise virgin who acts upon the Word of God. She is the church that has been made holy and blameless.

The other supper is described in verses 17 and 18 and God is serving this supper to the powers of darkness. These birds that fly in mid-heaven are the vultures, the consecrated guests, and the army that God will use to destroy and eat the flesh of the Babylon Harlot.

Revelation tells us: "Fallen, fallen is Babylon the great! And she has become a dwelling place of demons ... To the degree that she has glorified herself (pride) and lived sensuously, to the same degree give her torment and mourning ... And I heard another voice from heaven, saying, 'Come out of her, My people, that you may not participate in her sins and that you may not receive of her plagues' " (Rev. 18:2, 7, 4). Babylon is the residence of the foolish virgins. The wise virgins "... know that, when He appears, we shall be like Him ... and everyone who has this hope fixed on Him purifies himself ..." (I John 3:2, 3). "For God has not called us for the purpose of impurity, but in sanctification (pure heart). Consequently, he who rejects this is not rejecting man, but God ..." (I Thess. 4:7, 8).

Jesus Christ is now saying to those who can hear and understand: "Get ready (purify yourselves), come out to meet the Bridegroom." The foolish virgins whose hearts are already tied to carnal doctrines will not hear. As this shaking, destruction, and pressure increases, the foolish virgins will come to the wise virgins and want some of their oil because they cannot understand what is going on: "And the foolish (virgins) said to the prudent, 'Give us some of your oil, for our lamps are going out.' (We can't see what you see and we are being destroyed)" (Matt. 25:8).

Job explains: "Indeed, *the light of the wicked goes out,* and the flame of his fire gives no light. *The light in his tent (temple) is darkened, and his lamp goes out above him (no oil, Spirit of God).* His vigorous stride is shortened (by sickness and disease), and his own scheme (of the flesh) brings him down. For he is thrown into a net by his own feet ... a noose for him is hidden in the ground, and a trap for him on the path. *All around terrors (powers of darkness) frighten him,* and harry him (oppression) at every step. His strength is famished, and calamity is ready at his side. His skin is devoured by disease, *the first born of death (Satan) devours his limbs.* He is torn from the security of his tent, and they (powers of darkness) march him before the king of terrors (Satan). *His roots are dried below and his branch is cut off above (from God). HE IS DRIVEN FROM LIGHT INTO DARKNESS, AND CHASED FROM THE INHABITED WORLD (DESTROYED).* Surely such are the dwellings of the wicked, and this is the place of him who does not know God" (Job 18:5-8, 10-14, 16, 18, 21).

This is the foolish virgin who asks the wise virgin for oil (Spirit), because she was being destroyed. But she did not understand until it was too late.

In Matthew we read: "But the prudent answered, 'No, there will not be enough for us and you too; go instead to the dealers and buy some for yourselves.' And while they (the foolish virgins) were going away to make the purchase, the *BRIDEGROOM CAME,* and *those (wise virgins) who WERE READY went in (THE ARK, JESUS CHRIST)* with Him to the *WEDDING FEAST;* and the *DOOR WAS SHUT* (as it was in the days of Noah)" (Matt. 25:9, 10).

A worldly church has its mind set on earthly things. Its heart is tied to the world and the things in the world: this is the reason they will not come into the ark with Christ to the wedding feast. "The kingdom of heaven may be compared to a king, who gave a wedding feast for his son. And he sent out his slaves to call those (out of the world) who had been invited to the wedding feast, and they were unwilling to come" (Matt. 22:2, 3). "But they all alike began to make excuses. The first one said to him, 'I have bought a piece of land and I need to go out and look at it; please consider me excused (God).' And another one said, 'I have bought five yoke of oxen, and I am going to try them out; please consider me excused (God).' And another one said, 'I have married a wife, and for that reason I cannot come' (God)" (Luke 14:18-20).

Matthew added: "Again he sent out other slaves saying, 'Tell those who have been invited, Behold, I have prepared my dinner; my oxen and my fattened livestock are all butchered and everything is ready; come to the wedding feast.' But they paid no attention and went their own way (of the flesh and the world), one to his farm, another to his business, and the rest seized his slaves and mistreated them and killed them. But the *king* (Jesus) was *enraged* and *SENT HIS ARMIES* (the powers of darkness no longer restrained), and *DESTROYED* those murderers, and *SET THEIR CITIES (WORLD AND CHURCHES) ON FIRE*. Then he said to his slaves, The wedding is ready, but those who were invited *were not worthy* (because they chose to love the world and the nature of Satan)' " (Matt. 22:4-8).

Luke added: " 'For I tell you, none of these men who were invited shall taste of my dinner. If anyone comes to Me, and does not hate (love less) his own father and mother and wife and children and brothers and sisters, yes, and even his own (fleshly) life, he cannot be My disciple. Whoever does not carry his own cross (deny himself) and come after Me cannot be My disciple' " (Luke 14:24, 26, 27).

Again, Matthew wrote: "And later the other virgins (false church) also came, saying, 'Lord, Lord, open up for us.' But He answered and said ' … I do not know you' " (Matt. 25:11, 12).

These are the same foolish virgins in Matthew 7:21 who were led astray by false prophets. They will say, 'Lord, Lord,' thinking Jesus Christ is their Lord, but they did not do the will of the Father. *These are the ones who do not get ready and do not purify their hearts, but bear the fruit of a form of godliness.* They will try to get through the small gate and the narrow way, but will not find it because they are evildoers who bear the wrong fruit.

Listen again to the words of Luke: "And someone said to Him, 'Lord, are there just a few who are being saved?' And He said to them, 'Strive to enter by the narrow door; for *many,* I tell you, will seek to enter, and will not be able. Once the head of the house gets up and shuts the door *(to the ark, Jesus Christ),* and you begin to stand outside and knock (by praying) on the door (to Jesus Christ), saying, 'Lord, open up to us!' Then He will answer and say to you, 'I do not know where you are from.' Then you will begin to say, 'We (the foolish virgins) ate and drank in your presence, and you taught in our streets'; and He will say, 'I tell you, I do not know where you are from; depart from Me, all you *evildoers* (who bear the wrong fruit)' " (Luke 13:23-27).

The Apostle Paul wrote: "Now the deeds of the flesh are evident, which are: immorality, impurity, sensuality, idolatry, sorcery, enmities, strife, jealousy ... and things like these, of which I forewarn you, just as I have forewarned you that *those who practice such things shall not inherit the kingdom of God."* (Gal. 5:19-21).

The body of Christ, the wise virgins, purify their hearts and die to the flesh nature in order to bear the fruit of love, the nature of God.

The prophet Amos wrote: "She has fallen, she will not rise again — the (foolish) virgin Israel ... There is none to raise her up. For thus says the Lord God, 'The city which goes forth a *thousand strong* will have a *hundred left,* and the one which goes forth a *hundred strong* will have *ten left* to the house of Israel (remnant). Seek the Lord that you may live, lest He break forth like a *fire,* O house of Joseph (church)...for those who turn justice into wormwood (fruit of the flesh) and cast righteousness down to the earth. He who...calls for the water of the sea (flood) and pours them out on the surface of the earth, the Lord is His name. It is He who flashes forth (like lightning) with destruction upon the strong (after the works of the flesh) so the destruction comes upon the fortress (fortified cities)" (Amos 5:2,3, 6-9).

Amos also said: "They hate him who reproves in the gate...Alas, you who are longing for the day of the Lord, for what purpose will the day of the Lord be to you? It will be darkness and not light; as when a man flees from a lion, and a bear meets him...will not the day of the Lord be (spiritual) darkness instead of light...Woe to those who are at ease in Zion; and to those who feel secure...the distinguished men (of pride)...to whom the house of Israel comes...yet they have not grieved over the ruin of Joseph (the church)" (Amos 5:10, 18-20; 6:1, 6).

Jeremiah wrote: "Why then has this people, Jerusalem, turned away in continual apostasy? They hold fast to deceit, they refuse to return (repent). I have listened and heard, they have spoken what is not right...everyone turned to his course. How can you say, 'We are WISE and the law of the Lord is with us?' But behold, the lying pen of the scribes (writers of religious literature) has made it into a lie...Behold, they have rejected the word of the Lord, and what kind of wisdom do they have?" (Jer. 8:5, 6, 8, 9)

Jeremiah also pointed out: "...Everyone is greedy for gain, and from the prophet even to the priest, everyone deals falsely. And they have healed the brokenness of My people superficially, saying 'Peace, peace,' but there is no peace. Were they ashamed because of the abominations they have done? ...They did not even know how to blush. Therefore they shall fall among those who fall; at the time that I punish them, they shall be cast down,' says the Lord" (Jer. 6:13, 15). "Thus says the Lord, 'Stand by the ways and see and ask for the ancient paths, where the good way is (covenant), and *walk in it;* and you will find rest (and peace) for your souls.' But they said, 'We will not walk in it.' And I set watchmen over you, saying, *'LISTEN TO THE SOUND OF THE TRUMPET!' (TODAY)* But they said, 'We will not listen.' Therefore hear, O nations, and know, O congregation ... behold, I am bringing *disaster* on this people, the fruit of their plans, because they have not listened to My words" (Jer. 6:16-19).

This is the fate of the foolish virgins who preach "peace and safety."

God is now giving light and understanding about these last days to the wise virgins. They will respond immediately to the call of God's trumpet: "... Brethren (wise virgins), you have no need of anything to be written to you. For you (brethren) yourselves know full well that the day of the Lord will come just like a *thief* in the *night.* While they (foolish virgins) are saying (preaching), 'Peace and safety!' then *destruction* will come upon *THEM* (who preach peace and safety) suddenly *like birth pangs upon a woman* with child; and they shall not escape. But you, brethren, are not in (spiritual) darkness, that the day (of the Lord) should overtake you like a thief" (I Thess. 5:1-4).

Babylon, the Great Harlot

God's judgment is upon the foolish virgins who are not obeying the Word of God. In many places the scriptures refer to these foolish virgins as the harlot. This great harlot is also known as Babylon! "... *Come here, I shall show you the judgment of the great harlot* who sits on many waters. Because His judgments are true and righteous; for He has judged the great harlot who was corrupting the earth with her immorality ..." (Rev. 17:1; 19:2).

Jeremiah said: "Declare and proclaim among the nations ... *Babylon (the harlot church) has been captured* ... My people have become lost sheep; *their shepherds have led them astray* ... All (the powers of darkness) who came upon them have devoured them; and their adversaries have said, 'We are not guilty,' inasmuch as they have sinned against the Lord (broken God's law) ... For behold, I am going to arouse and bring up against Babylon *a horde of great nations* ... and they will draw up their *battle lines* against her; from there she will be *taken captive* ... Draw up your battle lines against Babylon on every side ... for she has sinned against the Lord" (Jer. 50:2, 6, 7, 9, 14).

"The Lord has opened His *armory* and has brought forth the *weapons of His indignation* (proud exulting ones) ... Summon many against Babylon ... repay her according to her work ... according to all that she has done, so do to her (by her standard of measure, measure unto her); for she has become arrogant ... against the Holy One of Israel (Jesus Christ). Behold, a people is coming from the north, and a great nation and many kings will be *aroused* from the remote parts of the earth ... They are cruel and have no mercy. *Their voice roars like the sea* ... therefore hear the plan of the Lord which He has planned against Babylon ... At the shout, 'Babylon has been seized!' the earth is shaken (earthquake), and an outcry is heard among the nations" (Jer. 50:25, 39, 41, 42, 45, 46).

Jeremiah also wrote: "Thus says the Lord, 'Behold, I am going to arouse against Babylon ... the spirit of a destroyer ... for on every side they will be opposed to her (this is the army that is surrounding Jerusalem today) in the day of her calamity. Flee from the midst of Babylon and each of you save his life! Do not be destroyed in her punishment, for this is the Lord's time of vengeance ... sharpen the arrows, fill the quivers! ... *because His purpose is against Babylon (the harlot church) to destroy it;* for it is the *vengeance* of the Lord, *vengeance for His temple* ... Surely I will fill you with a population like *locusts* (powers of darkness) and they will cry out with shouts of victory over you.' He says, 'You (powers of darkness) are my warclub, My weapon of war; and with you I shatter nations, and with you I destroy kingdoms. *And with you (powers of darkness) I shatter the shepherd and his flock ...*" (Jer. 51:1, 2, 6, 11, 14, 20, 23).

Jeremiah continued: "So the *LAND QUAKES* (the powers of darkness come against all foundations that are sand, this is the spiritual earthquake) ... for the purposes of the Lord against Babylon stand, to make the land of Babylon (the harlot church) a *desolation* (the powers of darkness are the abomination that makes desolation) ... The mighty men of Babylon have ceased fighting (they no longer go to the breaches) ... *Their dwelling places are set on fire,* the bars of her gate are broken. 'When they (harlot church today) become heated up, I shall serve them their banquet and make them drunk (staggering in spiritual darkness), that they may become jubilant and *may sleep a perpetual sleep and not wake up,'* declares the Lord. *'THE SEA (FLOOD) HAS COME UP OVER BABYLON;* she has become engulfed with its tumultuous waves. Come forth from her midst, My people, and each of you save yourselves from the fierce anger of the Lord ... Disgrace has covered our faces, *FOR ALIENS* (the powers of darkness) *HAVE ENTERED THE HOLY PLACES (temples) OF THE LORD'S HOUSE.* For the destroyer is coming against her, against Babylon, and her mighty men will be captured ... for the Lord is a God of recompense, He will fully repay. And I will make her princes (leaders) and her wise men drunk (spiritual darkness) ... *that they may sleep a perpetual sleep and not wake up,' declares the KING (the Lord Jesus Christ) WHOSE NAME IS THE LORD OF HOSTS*" (Jer. 51:29, 30, 39, 42, 45, 51, 56, 57).

"... So the peoples will toil for nothing, and the nations become exhausted only for fire. And it will come about as soon as you finish reading this scroll, you will tie a stone to it and throw it into the middle of the Euphrates, and say, 'Just so shall Babylon (the harlot church) sink down and not rise again, because of the calamity that I am going to bring upon her; and they will become exhausted. ...' " (Jer. 51:58, 63, 64).

"Woe to the world because of *stumbling blocks!* For it is inevitable that *stumbling blocks* come; but woe to that man through whom the stumbling block comes! ... it is better for him that a *heavy millstone* be hung around his neck, and that he be *drowned in the depth of the sea.*" (Matt. 18:7, 6).

Babylon the harlot has become a curse and a stumbling-block to almost everyone in the world who has tried to come to God. Instead of teaching God's little ones righteousness and holiness, they have perverted the Word and instructed them falsely in order to fulfill selfish ambition and build a fleshly kingdom for Satan. Satan is the king over Babylon.

The Apostle John wrote in Revelation: "Rejoice over her, O heaven, and you (true) saints and (true) apostles and (true) prophets, because God has *pronounced judgment* for you against her. And a strong angel took up a stone like a *GREAT MILLSTONE* and threw it into the SEA, saying, 'Thus will Babylon (the harlot church), the great city (of stumbling-blocks), be thrown down with *violence* (flood of destruction), and will not be found any longer (destroyed). And the *light of a lamp* will not shine in you any longer (no Spirit, no Word); and the voice of the *bridegroom* (Jesus) and the *bride* will not be heard in you any longer ... because all the nations were deceived by your sorcery. And in her was found ... all who have been slain on the earth" (Rev. 18:20, 21, 23, 24).

The Psalmist said: "Save me, O God, for the waters have threatened my life. I have sunk in deep mire, and there is no foothold (no foundation); *I have come into deep waters, and a flood overflows me.* I am weary with my crying; my throat is parched ... Those who hate me without a cause are more than the hairs of my head; those who would *destroy me* are powerful ... Deliver me from the mire, and do not let me sink; may I be delivered from my foes and from the deep waters, *May the flood of water not overflow me,* and may the deep not swallow me up, and may the pit not shut its mouth on me" (Ps. 69:1-4, 14, 15).

THE TRUMPET IS BLOWING.

Jesus warns us "... *when you see Jerusalem surrounded by armies* (we see this today), then recognize that her *desolation* is at hand. Let those who are in Judea flee to the mountains, and let those who are in the midst of the city depart (those who hear the trumpet will leave Babylon and go to Zion), and let not those who are in the country enter the city; because these are the *days of vengeance,* in order that all things which are written may be fulfilled. Woe to those who are with child and to those who nurse babes in those days; for there will be *great distress* upon the land, and *wrath to this people,* and they will *fall* by the edge of the *sword* (curse), and will be *led captive* into all the nations; and Jerusalem will be trampled underfoot by the (lost) Gentiles ..." (Luke 21:20-24).

Jesus also said: "And there will be signs in sun and moon and stars, and upon the earth dismay among nations, in perplexity at the *roaring of the sea* and the waves (of destruction), men fainting from fear and expectation of the things which are coming upon the world; for the powers of the heavens will be shaken. And then they will see the Son of Man coming in a cloud with power and great glory. But when these things begin to take place, straighten up and lift up your heads, because your redemption is drawing near" (Luke 21:25-28).

"Be on guard, that your *hearts* may not be weighted down with *dissipation* (pleasures of this life) and *drunkenness* (spiritual darkness) and the *worries of (this) life,* and that day (of the Lord) come on you like a *trap;* for it will come upon all those who dwell on the face of the earth. *But keep on the alert at all times, praying in order that you may have strength to escape (endure) all these things that are about to take place, and to stand before the Son of Man"* (Luke 21:34-36).

The Book of Revelation tells us: " 'Behold, I am coming like a thief. *Blessed* is the one who STAYS AWAKE (endures to the end) and KEEPS HIS GARMENTS (of salvation), lest he walk about *naked* and men see his shame'.) And there were flashes of lightning and sounds and peals of thunder; and there was a *great (spiritual) earthquake,* such as there had not been since man came to be upon the earth, so great an earthquake was it, and so mighty. And the great city (church) was split into three parts, and the cities of the nations (world) fell. And Babylon the great (harlot church) was remembered before God, to give her the cup of the wine of His fierce wrath" (Rev. 16:15, 18, 19).

THE TRUMPET IS BLOWING.

False Teachers and the Judgment of God

Listen to the Word of the Lord: "A jealous and avenging God is the Lord; the Lord is avenging and wrathful. The Lord takes vengeance on His adversaries, and He reserves wrath for His enemies. The Lord is slow to anger and great in power, and the Lord will by no means leave the guilty unpunished. In whirlwind and storm is His way ..." (Nahum 1:2, 3).

From Jeremiah we read: "Behold, the storm of the Lord has gone forth in wrath, even a whirling tempest; it will swirl down on the head of the wicked. The anger of the Lord will not turn back until He has performed and carried out the purposes of His heart; *in the last days you will clearly understand it.* 'I did not send these prophets, but they ran. I did not speak to them, but they prophesied. But if they had stood in My council, then they would have announced My words to My people, and would have turned them back from their evil way and from the evil of their deeds' " (Jer. 23:19-22).

Again, from Nahum: "Who can stand before His (instruments of) indignation? Who can endure the burning of His anger? His wrath is poured out like *fire* ... The Lord is good, a stronghold in the day of trouble, and *He knows those who take refuge in Him.* But with an *OVER-FLOWING FLOOD* He will make a complete end of its site, and will *pursue His enemies into darkness*. Like tangled thorns, and like those who are *drunken with their drink*, (stumbling in spiritual darkness) they are *consumed as stubble* completely withered. The Lord has issued a command concerning you: 'Your name will no longer be perpetuated. I will cut off idol and image from the house of your gods. *I will prepare your grave*, for you are contemptible' " (Nahum 1:6-8, 10, 14).

From Isaiah: "Therefore, hear the word of the Lord, O scoffers, who rule this people who are in Jerusalem (with false teaching), because you have said, 'We have made a covenant with death, and with Sheol we have made a pact (no curse can come on us). The overwhelming scourge (flood) will not reach us when it passes by, for *we have made falsehood our refuge and we have concealed ourselves with deception.*' Therefore thus says the Lord God, 'Behold, I am laying in Zion a stone, a tested stone, a costly cornerstone for the *foundation,* firmly placed. He who believes in it (stands on the foundation of the Word of God) will not be disturbed (he will be protected)" (Isa. 28:14-16).

"And I will make *justice* the measuring line, and *righteousness* the level; then hail shall sweep away the refuge of lies, and *the waters shall overflow (flood) the secret place.* And your covenant with death (false teaching) shall be canceled, and your pact with Sheol (that no calamity will come on you) shall not stand; when the overwhelming scourge (flood) passes through then you become its trampling place. As often as it (waves of destruction) passes through, it will seize you. For morning after morning it will pass through, anytime during the day or night. *And it will be sheer terror to understand what it means.*' And now do not carry on as scoffers, lest your fetters be made stronger; for I have heard from the Lord God of hosts, of decisive destruction on all the earth" (Isa. 28:17, 18, 19, 22).

THE TRUMPET IS BLOWING.

From Jeremiah: "For thus says the Lord, 'Your wound is incurable, and your injury is serious. There is no one (no advocate) to plead your cause; no healing for your sore, no recovery for you. ... For I have wounded you with the wound of an enemy, with the punishment of a cruel one ... why do you cry out over your injury? Your pain is incurable. Because your iniquity is great and your sins are numerous, *I have done these things to you*' " (Jer. 30:12-15).

Also from Jeremiah: "Behold, the tempest of the Lord! *Wrath* has gone forth, a sweeping tempest; it will burst on the head of the wicked. The fierce anger of the Lord will not turn back, until He has performed, and until He has accomplished the intent of His heart; *in the latter days you will understand this*" (Jer. 30:23, 24).

Once again from Nahum: " 'Woe to the bloody city (the harlot church), completely full of lies and pillage; her prey never departs. All because of the many harlotries of the harlot, the charming one, the mistress of sorceries, who sells nations by her harlotries and families by her sorceries. 'Behold, *I AM AGAINST YOU*,' declares the Lord of hosts; '*And I will lift up your skirts over your face*, and show to the *nations (world) your nakedness (lostness) and to the kingdoms your disgrace* ... The gates of your land are opened wide to your enemies; *fire* consumes your gate bars. There *fire will consume you*, the sword (the curse and tree cutters) will *cut you down;* it will consume you *as the locust does* ... *your shepherds are sleeping*, O king of Assyria; *Your nobles are lying down*. Your people are *scattered on the mountains*, and there is no one to regather them. There is no relief for your breakdown, your wound is incurable. All who hear about you clap their hands over you, for on whom has not your evil passed continually?' " (Nahum 3:1, 4, 5, 13, 15, 18, 19).

From Revelation: "And the fifth angel sounded, and I saw a star from heaven which had fallen to the earth; and the key of the bottomless pit was given to him. And out of the smoke came forth locusts (powers of darkness) upon the earth; and power was given them, as the scorpions of the earth have power. And in those days men will seek death and will not find it; and they will long to die (because of extreme pain, extreme fear, extreme depression, weakness, sickness, confusion, worry, discouragement, self pity, etc.) and death flees from them. They have as king over them, the angel of the abyss (Satan); his name in Hebrew is Abaddon (destruction), and in the Greek he has the name of Apollon (destroyer)" (Rev. 9:1, 3, 6, 11).

"And the four angels, who had been prepared for the hour and day and month and year, were released, so that they might kill a third of mankind. A third of mankind was killed by these three plagues, by the fire and the smoke and the brimstone, which proceeded out of their mouths. And the rest of mankind, who were not killed by these plagues, *did not repent of the works of their hands, so as not to worship demons,* and the *idols* of gold and silver and of brass and of stone and of wood, which can neither see nor hear nor walk; and they did *not repent* of their *murders* nor of their *sorceries* nor of their *immorality* nor of their *thefts*" (Rev. 9:15, 18, 20, 21).

From Jeremiah: "Hear this, O elders, and listen, all inhabitants of the land. Has anything like this happened in your days or your fathers' days? What the gnawing locust has left, the swarming locust has eaten; and what the swarming locust has left, the creeping locust has eaten; and what the creeping locust has left, the stripping locust has eaten. *AWAKE, DRUNKARDS* (who are stumbling in spiritual darkness), and weep; and wail, all you wine drinkers, on account of the sweet wine (Word of God) that is cut off from your mouth (famine of the Word). For a nation (powers of darkness) has invaded my land, mighty and without number; its teeth are the teeth of a *lion,* and it has the fangs of a lioness. *Wail like a virgin girded with sackcloth for the BRIDEGROOM OF HER YOUTH* (their first love, Jesus) ... The field is ruined (hardened hearts), the land mourns (curse), for the grain is ruined (no fruit), the new wine dries up (famine of the Word), fresh oil fails (no anointing of the Holy Spirit)" (Jer. 1:2-10).

Joel is speaking to us today: "Consecrate a fast, proclaim a solemn assembly; gather the elders and all the inhabitants of the land to the house of the Lord your God, and *cry out to the Lord.* Alas for the day! For *the day of the Lord is near,* and it will come as *destruction* from the Almighty. Has not food (the Word) been cut off before our eyes, *gladness* and *joy* from the house of our God? The seeds (Word of God) shrivel under the clods (hardened hearts); the storehouses are desolate, the barns are torn down, for the grain (fruit) is dried up. To Thee, O Lord, I cry; for *FIRE HAS DEVOURED THE PASTURES* of the wilderness, and *THE FLAME HAS BURNED UP ALL THE TREES OF THE FIELD"* (Joel 1:14-20).

Also from Joel: *"BLOW A TRUMPET IN ZION, AND SOUND AN ALARM ON MY HOLY MOUNTAIN!* Let all inhabitants of the land tremble, for the day of the Lord is coming; surely it is near, *a day of (spiritual) darkness and gloom,* a day of clouds and thick darkness. As the dawn is spread over the mountains, so there is a great and mighty people; *THERE HAS NEVER BEEN ANYTHING LIKE IT,* nor will there be again after it to the years of many generations. A *fire consumes* before them, and behind them a *flame burns.* The land is like the garden of Eden before them, but a desolate wilderness is behind them ..." (Joel 2:1-3).

Again from Joel: "Before them the people are in *anguish;* all faces turn *pale* (weakness and fear). They run like mighty men (an army); they climb the (whitewashed) wall like soldiers; and they each march in line, nor do they deviate from their paths. They do not crowd each other; they march everyone in his path. When they burst through the defenses, they do not break ranks. They rush on the city (church), they run on the wall (false hedge); they climb into the houses (bodies, temples), they enter through the windows like a *thief.* Before them the *earth quakes* (shaking foundations), the heavens tremble, the sun and the moon grow dark, and the stars lose their brightness (spiritual darkness). And *the Lord utters His voice (shout) before His army (of destruction) ...*" (Joel 2:6-11).

THE TRUMPET IS BLOWING.

From Isaiah: "The Lord will go forth like a warrior, He will arouse His zeal like a man of war. He will *UTTER A SHOUT*, yes, He will raise a war cry. He will prevail against His enemies. I have kept silent for a long time. I have kept still and restrained Myself. Now like a woman in labor (pangs) I will groan, I will both gasp and pant. I will lay waste the mountains and hills, and wither all their vegetation ..." (Isa. 42:13-15).

From Lamentations: "The Lord has become like an enemy, He has swallowed up Israel; He has swallowed up all its *palaces;* He has destroyed its strongholds and multiplied in the daughter of Judah mourning and moaning" (Lam. 2:5).

From Jeremiah: "But, 'Ah, Lord God!' I said, *'Look, the prophets are telling* them,' You will not see the sword (curse) nor will you have famine (of the word), but I will give you lasting peace in this place.' Then the Lord said to me, 'The prophets are prophesying falsehood in My name. I have neither sent them nor commanded them nor spoken to them; they are prophesying to you a false vision, divination, futility, and the deception of their own minds.' Therefore thus says the Lord concerning the prophets who are prophesying in My name, although it was not I who sent them — yet they keep saying, 'There shall be no sword (no curse) or famine in this land' — *BY SWORD AND FAMINE THESE PROPHETS SHALL MEET THEIR END!'* " (Jer. 14:13-15).

Also from Jeremiah: " 'I have forsaken My house, I have abandoned My inheritance; *I have given the beloved of My soul into the hand of her enemies.* My inheritance has become to Me like a lion in the forest; she has roared against Me; therefore I have come to *HATE HER.* Is My inheritance like a speckled bird of prey to Me? Are the birds of prey (powers of darkness) against her on every side? Go gather all the beasts of the field, bring them to devour! *MANY SHEPHERDS HAVE RUINED MY VINEYARD (My church)*, they have trampled down My field; they have made My pleasant field a desolate wilderness' " (Jer. 12:7-10).

From Isaiah: " 'All you beasts of the field (powers of darkness), all you beasts in the forest, come to eat. His watchmen are blind, all of them know nothing. All of them are dumb dogs unable to bark (preach righteousness and judgment), dreamers (foolish virgins) lying down who love to slumber (sleep); and the dogs are greedy, they are not satisfied. And they are *SHEPHERDS WHO HAVE NO UNDERSTANDING:* they have all *turned to their own way*, each one to his unjust gain (after the flesh), to the last one' " (Isa. 56:9-11).

Also from Isaiah: "O people in Zion, inhabitant in Jerusalem, you will weep no longer. He will surely be gracious to you at the sound of your cry; when He hears it, He will answer you. Although the Lord has given you bread of privation and water of oppression, He, your teacher will no longer hide Himself, but your eyes will behold your Teacher. And your ears will hear a word behind you, 'This is the way, walk in it,' whenever you turn to the right or to the left" (Isa. 30:19-21).

Again, from Isaiah: "Then He will give you rain for the seed which you will sow in the ground, and bread from the yield of the ground, and it will be rich and plenteous; on that day your livestock will graze in a roomy pasture. And on every lofty mountain and on every high hill there will be streams running with water *on the day of the great slaughter, when the towers fall*. And the light of the moon will be as the light of the sun, and the light of the sun will be seven times brighter, like the light of seven days, on the day the Lord binds up the fracture of His people and heals the bruise He has inflicted" (Isa. 30:23, 25, 26).

From Jeremiah: " 'Only acknowledge your iniquity, that you have transgressed against the Lord your God and have scattered your favors to the strangers under every green tree, and you have not obeyed My voice,' declares the Lord. 'Return, O faithless sons,' declares the Lord. 'For I am a master to you. And I will take you one from a city and two from a family, and I will bring you to Zion' " (Jer. 3:13, 14).

From Isaiah: " 'Surely, as a woman treacherously departs from her lover, so you have dealt treacherously with Me, O house of Israel,' declares the Lord. 'Return, O faithless sons, I will heal your faithlessness.' 'Behold, we come to Thee; for Thou art the Lord our God.' " (Jeremiah 3:20, 22). " 'The One forming light and creating darkness, causing well-being and creating calamity; I am the Lord who does all these things' " (Isa. 45:7).

"And the Lord said to him, 'Go through the midst of the city, even through the midst of Jerusalem (church), and *put a mark on the foreheads of the men who sigh and groan over all the abominations which are being committed in its midst.*' But to the others (instruments of indignation) He said in my hearing, 'Go through the city after him and strike ... utterly slay old men, young men, maidens, little children, and women, but do not touch any man on whom is the mark; and you shall *start from My sanctuary.*' So they started with the *elders* who were before the temple" (Ezek. 9:4-6).

"Then it came about as they were striking and I alone was left, that I fell on my face and cried out saying, 'Alas, Lord God! Art Thou destroying the whole remnant of Israel by pouring out Thy wrath (flood) on Jerusalem?' Then He said to me, 'The *iniquity* of the house of Israel and Judah is *VERY, VERY GREAT,* and the land is filled with blood, and the city is full of perversion; for they say, 'The Lord has forsaken the land, and the Lord does not see!' But as for Me, My eye will have no pity nor shall I spare, but I shall bring their conduct upon their heads' " (Ezek. 9:8-10).

From Joel: "... The Lord utters His voice (shout) before His *army (of destruction);* surely His camp is very great, for strong is He who carries out His word. The day of the Lord is indeed great and very awesome, and who can endure it?

'Yet even now,' declares the Lord, 'Return to Me with all your heart, and with fasting, weeping, and mourning; and rend your heart and not your garments.' Now return to the Lord your God, for He is gracious and compassionate, slow to anger, abounding in lovingkindness, and relenting of evil" (Joel 2:11-13).

From Isaiah: *"BLOW A TRUMPET IN ZION,* consecrate a fast, proclaim a solemn assembly, gather the people, *sanctify the congregation,* assemble the elders, gather the children and the nursing infants. Let the *BRIDEGROOM* (Jesus) come out of His room and the *BRIDE* (the body of Christ) out of her bridal chamber. Let the priests, the Lord's ministers, weep between the porch and the altar, and let them say, 'Spare Thy people, O Lord, and do not make Thine inheritance a reproach, a byword among the nations. Why should they among peoples say,' 'Where is their God?' " (Joel 2:15-17). "... The ambassadors of peace (the church) weep bitterly. The *highways (of holiness)* are desolate, the traveler (who walks in holiness) has ceased, he has *broken the covenant,* he has despised the cities, he has no regard for man (he does not love his neighbor)" (Isa. 33:7, 8).

Also from Isaiah: "You have conceived chaff, you will give birth to *stubble;* My breath will consume you like a *fire* (God speaks judgment). Sinners in Zion are terrified; trembling has seized the godless (weakness and fear). Who among us can live with the *consuming fire?* Who among us can live with *continual burning?* He who walks righteously (has a hedge to protect him from the enemy), and speaks with sincerity, he who rejects unjust gain (no selfishness), and shakes his hands so that they hold no bribe (no greed); he who stops his ears from hearing about bloodshed, and shuts his eyes from looking upon evil; he will dwell on the heights; his *refuge* will be the *impregnable rock (Jesus);* his bread (Word) will be given him; his water will be sure" (Isa. 33:11, 14-16).

Again from Isaiah: "Your eyes will see the King in His beauty; they will behold a far-distant land (as they look back on the people still in bondage). Your heart will meditate on terror (their destruction): 'Where is he who counts (his numbers and achievements)? Where is he who weighs (the gold, the money)? Where is he who counts the (high corner) towers?' " (They have been destroyed) (Isa. 33:17, 18).

From Joel: "... The Lord will be zealous for His land, and will have pity on His people. And the Lord will answer and say to His people, 'Behold, I am going to send you grain (fruit), new wine (Word), and oil (Spirit), and you will be satisfied in full with them; and I will never again make you a reproach among the nations. But I will remove the northern army (powers of darkness) far from you, and I will drive it into a parched and desolate land (dry places) ... So rejoice, O sons of Zion, and be glad in the Lord your God; for He has given you the early rain for your vindication and He has poured down for you rain, the early and latter rain as before (restoration). *Then I will make up to you for the years that the swarming locust (powers of darkness) has eaten,* the creeping locust, the stripping locust, and the gnawing locust, *MY GREAT ARMY WHICH I SENT AMONG YOU"* (Joel 2:18-20, 23, 25).

From Isaiah: "Awake, awake, clothe yourself in your strength, O Zion. Clothe yourself in your beautiful garments, O Jerusalem, the holy city. For the uncircumcised and the unclean will no more come into you. Shake yourself from the dust, rise up, O captive Jerusalem; loose yourself from the chains around your neck, O captive daughter of Zion," (Isa. 52:1, 2).

From Daniel: "Now at that time Michael, the great prince who stands guard over the sons of your people, will arise. And there will be a time of distress such as never occurred since there was a nation until that time; and at that time your people, everyone who is found written in the book, will be rescued. And those who have insight will shine brightly like the brightness of the expanse of heaven, and those who lead the many to righteousness, like the stars forever and ever. But as for you, Daniel, conceal these words and seal up the book until the end of time ... and *knowledge will increase.* ... Go your way, Daniel, for these words are concealed and sealed up until the end time. Many will be purged, purified, and refined; but the wicked will act wickedly, and *none of the wicked will understand, but those who have insight will understand"* (Dan. 12:1, 3, 4, 9, 10).

10

Rebuilding the Temple In the Last Days

Matthew wrote: "And Jesus came out from the temple and was going away when His disciples came up to point out the *temple buildings* to Him. And He answered and said to them, 'Do you not see all these things? Truly I say to you, not one *stone* here shall be left upon another, which will not be torn down.' And as He was sitting on the Mount of Olives, the *disciples* came to Him *privately,* saying, 'Tell us, when will these things be, and what will be the sign of your coming, and the end of the age?' " (Matt. 24:1-3).

Matthew also recorded: "And Jesus answered and said to them, 'See to it that no one *misleads you* (with false teaching). For many will come in My name, saying, 'I am the Christ,' and will *mislead many* ... in various places there will be *FAMINES* and *EARTHQUAKES.* But all these things are merely the *BEGINNING OF BIRTH PANGS* (destruction). And at that time *many will FALL AWAY* and will deliver up one another and *hate one another.* And many *FALSE PROPHETS* will arise, and will mislead many. And because *LAWLESSNESS IS INCREASED,* most people's love will grow cold. *But the one who endures to the end, he shall be saved.* And *THIS GOSPEL* of the kingdom shall be preached in the whole world for a witness to all the nations, and *then the end shall come'* " (Matt. 24:4, 5, 7, 8, 10, 14).

Again, Matthew said: " 'Therefore when you see the ABOMINATION OF DESOLATION (powers of darkness) which was spoken of through Daniel the prophet, STANDING IN THE HOLY PLACE (the bodies of men are God's temples) [Let the reader understand], ... For then there will be a GREAT TRIBULATION, such as has not occurred since the beginning of the world until now, nor ever shall. Then if anyone says to you, 'Behold, here is the (body) of Christ,' or 'There He is,' do not believe him. For false Christs and false prophets will arise and will show great signs and wonders, so as to mislead, if possible, even the elect' " (Matt. 24:15, 21, 23, 24).

Peter wrote: "For this is contained in scripture: 'Behold I lay in Zion a choice stone, *a precious corner stone,* and he who believes in Him shall not be disappointed.' This precious value, then, is for you who believe. But for those who disbelieve, 'The *stone* which the builders rejected, this became the very *cornerstone,*' and, 'a stone of stumbling and a rock of offense' ..." (I Pet. 2:6-8).

The elect of God will come to Jesus "... as to a living stone, rejected by men, but choice and precious in the sight of God, you also, as *LIVING STONES, are being built up as a SPIRITUAL HOUSE (THE TEMPLE OF GOD) for a holy priesthood,* to offer up spiritual sacrifices acceptable to God through Jesus Christ" (I Pet. 2:4, 5).

The remnant will be living stones which are the members of the body of Christ which are used to build the temple of God," ... having been built upon the *foundation* of the apostles and prophets, Christ Jesus Himself being the *corner stone,* in whom the *WHOLE BUILDING,* being *FITTED TOGETHER* is growing into a HOLY TEMPLE in the Lord: in whom *you also* are being *built together into a dwelling of God in the Spirit*" (Eph. 2:20-22).

The building of the temple today is the responsibility of the craftsmen, the *true* apostles, prophets, evangelists, pastors, and teachers "for the equipping of the saints ... to the building up of the body of Christ ... from whom the *whole body, being fitted and held together* by that which every joint (member) supplies ... causes the growth of the (spiritual) body for the *building up of itself in love,* until we all attain to the unity of the faith ... to a mature man to the (same) measure of the stature which belongs to the fullness of Christ" (Eph. 4:12, 16, 13).

This body of Christ becomes the temple of God because it is the exact representation of the measure and stature of the fulness of Christ: "For we are God's fellow workers; you are God's field, *GOD'S BUILDING"* (I Cor. 3:9).

Mark wrote: "And as He was going out of the temple, one of His disciples said to Him, 'Teacher, behold what *wonderful stones* and what *wonderful buildings!'* And Jesus said to him, 'Do you see these great buildings? Not one stone shall be left upon another which will not be torn down (Jesus is building a new temple)" (Mark 13:1, 2).

False teachers still admire and build beautiful buildings for God while the true craftsmen will build up and fit together the body of Christ in love.

From Amos: "For behold, I am commanding, and I will *shake* (the foundations of) the house of Jacob among all nations as grain is shaken in a sieve, but not a kernel will fall to the ground. All the sinners of My people will die by the sword (curse), those who say, 'The calamity will not overtake or confront us.' In that day I will raise up the fallen booth of David, and wall up its breaches; I will also raise up its ruins, and rebuild it as in the days of old" (Amos 9:9-11).

As the law had been lost in the day of Ezra and Nehemiah, it has been lost to us today. They found themselves in disobedience to God's law as we have found ourselves in disobedience to God's law today. Their wall (hedge of protection) was gone and they had been led into captivity as we are today. God's grace brought reviving and restoration so they could rebuild the wall and the house of God in the midst of distress. The temple today will also be built in the midst of distress and opposition. This is "an example for our instruction" to rebuild the wall (hedge) and temple today.

Ezra wrote: "BUT NOW FOR A *BRIEF MOMENT GRACE* HAS BEEN SHOWN FROM THE LORD OUR GOD, TO LEAVE US AN *ESCAPED REMNANT* and to give us a peg in His holy place (Jesus Christ), that our God may *enlighten our eyes* (understanding) and grant us a *little reviving* (revival) in our bondage" (Ezra 9:8).

For just as God granted them a brief moment of grace, He is doing the same today to give us understanding to escape the traditions and the bondage of a harlot church (Babylon) and the powers of darkness: "For we are slaves; yet in our bondage, our God has not forsaken us, but has extended lovingkindness to us in the sight of the kings of Persia, to give us *reviving* to raise up the house of God (the temple), to restore its ruins, and to give us a wall (hedge) in Judah and Jerusalem" (Ezra 9:9).

Nehemiah wrote: "And all the people gathered as one man at the square which was in front of the Water Gate, and they asked Ezra the scribe to bring the *book of the law of Moses* which the Lord had given to Israel. And Ezra the scribe stood at a wooden podium which they had made for the purpose ... And Ezra opened the book in the sight of all the people for he was standing above all the people; and when he opened it, all the people stood up (in reverence to the Word of God). Then Ezra blessed the Lord the great God. And all the people answered, 'Amen, Amen!' while lifting up their hands; then they bowed low and worshiped the Lord with their faces to the ground" (Neh. 8:1, 4-6).

Nehemiah also wrote: "And they read from the book, for the *law of God,* translating to give the sense so that they understood the reading. Then Nehemiah, who was the governor, and Ezra the priest and scribe, and the Levites who taught the people said to all the people, 'This day is holy to the Lord your God; do not mourn or weep.' For all the people were weeping (in repentance) when they heard the words of the law" (Neh. 8:8, 9).

The Lord is giving His remnant understanding as He did then. When the people began to have understanding of the law, they saw the darkness and sin they had been living in and began to repent.

Again from Nehemiah: "... the sons of Israel assembled with *fasting,* in sackcloth, and with dirt upon them. And the descendants of Israel (remnant) separated themselves from all foreigners, and stood and confessed their sins and iniquities of their fathers. While they stood in their place, they read from the book of the law of the Lord their God for a fourth of the day; and for another fourth they confessed and worshiped the Lord their God" (Neh. 9:1-3).

Nehemiah added: "And they said to me, 'The remnant there in the province who *survived the captivity are in great distress and reproach,* and the wall (hedge) of Jerusalem is broken down and its *gates are burned with fire.*' And I said, 'I beseech Thee, O Lord God of heaven, the great and awesome God, who preserves the covenant and loving - kindness for those who love Him and keep His command - ments' ... 'We have acted very *corruptly* against Thee and *have not kept the commandments* ... which Thou didst command Thy servant Moses. Remember the word which Thou didst command Thy servant Moses, saying,' 'If you are unfaithful I will scatter you among the peoples (curses); but if you return to Me and keep My commandments and do them, though those of you who have been scattered were in the most remote part of the heavens, I will gather them from there and will bring them to the place where I have chosen to cause My name to dwell' " (Neh. 1:3, 5, 7-9).

The Lord's promise stands today to those who return and become doers of the law through Christ. God is gathering His elect today.

The remnant the Lord is calling out recognizes the ruin of Jerusalem, the desolate condition of the harlot church today: "Then I said to them, 'You see the bad condition we are in, that Jerusalem is *desolate* and its *gates burned by fire.* Come, let us *rebuild the wall* of Jerusalem that we may no longer be a reproach.' And I told them how the hand of my God had been favorable to me ... Then they said, 'LET US ARISE AND BUILD.' So they put their hands to the good work" (Neh. 2:17, 18).

From Ezra: "Now when the builders had laid the foundation of the temple of the Lord, the priests stood in their apparel with trumpets ... to praise the Lord ... And they sang, praising and giving thanks to the Lord ... And all the people shouted with a great shout when they praised the Lord, because the foundation of the house of the Lord was laid ... the old men who had seen the first temple, wept with a loud voice when the foundation of this house was laid before their eyes, while many shouted aloud for joy; so that the people could not distinguish the shout of joy from the sound of the weeping of the people ..." (Ezra 3:10-13).

Again from Ezra: "Now when the *enemies* of Judah and Benjamin heard that the people of the exile were building a temple to the Lord God of Israel, they approached ... and said to them, 'Let us (the harlot) build with you, for we, like you, seek your God' ... Zerubbabel and Jeshua and the rest of the heads of the fathers' households of Israel said to them, 'You have nothing in common with us in building a house to our God; but we ourselves will ... build to the Lord God of Israel ...' " (Ezra 4:1-3).

Once again from Ezra: "Rehum the commander and Shimshai the scribe wrote a letter *against Jerusalem* ... 'Let it be known to the king ... they are rebuilding the rebellious and evil city, and are finishing the walls and repairing the foundations. Now let it be known to the king, that if that city is rebuilt and the walls are finished, they will not *pay tribute (to the system),* custom or toll, and *it will damage the revenue of the kings*' " (Ezra 4:8, 12, 13).

From Nehemiah: "... When Sanballat the Horonite, and Tobiah the Ammonite official, and Geshem the Arab heard it, they mocked us and despised us and said, 'What is this thing you are doing? Are you rebelling against the king?' So I answered them and said to them, 'The God of heaven will give us success; therefore we His servants will arise and build, but you have no portion, right, or memorial in Jerusalem.' " (Neither will the ungodly have any part in building God's temple today) (Neh. 2:19, 20).

The false teachers who oppose restoration of God's real church today will be completely cut off unless they repent! Those who will not repent and come to God's light will become furious and angry as they see people leaving their flesh kingdoms to become a part of the remnant of restoration: "Now it came about that when Sanballat heard that we were rebuilding the wall, he became furious and very angry and mocked the Jews. And he spoke in the presence of his brothers and the wealthy men of Samaria (who were 'rich and increased with goods') and said, 'What are these feeble Jews doing? Are they going to restore it for themselves? ... Can they *revive the stones* (living stones) from the dusty rubble *EVEN THE BURNED ONES?* (The burned living stones are being revived today, those who have been burned by the fire of Satan)" (Neh. 4:1, 2).

"So the wall was completed ... And it came about when all our enemies heard of it, and all the nations surrounding us saw it, *they lost their confidence;* for they recognized that this work had been accomplished with the help of our God" (Neh 6:15, 16).

As God put it into the mind of an escaped remnant to rebuild the ruins in those days, God is doing the same today. The *temple and* the wall (hedge) is built today through repentance, and dealing with overcoming all sin in the body of Christ. This wall of protection is the Lord Jesus Christ: " 'For I,' declares the Lord, 'will be a wall of fire around her, and I will be the glory in her midst' " (Zech. 2:5). " 'And I will shake all the nations ... and I will fill this house with glory ... *the latter glory of this house will be greater than the former* ... and in this place I shall give peace (a wall),' declares the Lord of hosts" (Haggai 2:7, 9).

In the midst of these days of destruction, God's glory and power will be on the remnant as has never been in the history of mankind: "Behold, I will gather them out of all the lands to which I have driven them in My anger, in My wrath, and in great indignation; and I will bring them back to this place and make them dwell in safety. And they shall be My people, and I will be their God; and I will give them one heart and one way ..." (Jer. 32:37-39).

" 'At that time,' declares the Lord, 'I will be the God of all the families of Israel, and they shall be My people.' Thus says the Lord, 'The people who survived the sword (curse) found grace in the wilderness — Israel, when it went to find its rest.' The Lord appeared to him from afar, saying, 'I have loved you with an everlasting love; therefore *I have drawn you with lovingkindness.* Again I will build you, and you shall be rebuilt, O virgin of Israel! Again you shall take up your tambourines, and go forth to the dances of the merry-makers. For there shall be a day when *watchmen* on the hills of Ephraim shall call out,' *'ARISE, AND LET US GO UP TO ZION,* to the Lord our God.' 'For thus says the Lord,' 'Sing aloud with gladness for Jacob, and shout among the chiefs of the nations; proclaim, give praise, and say, 'O Lord, save Thy people, the remnant of Israel,' Behold, I am bringing them from the north country, and I will gather them from the remote parts of the earth ... they shall return here. With weeping they shall come, and by supplication I will lead them; I will make them walk by streams of waters, on a straight path in which they shall not stumble ... He who scattered Israel will gather him, and keep him as a shepherd keeps his flock. For the Lord has ransomed Jacob, and redeemed him from the hand of him who was stronger than he' " (Jer. 31:1-4, 6-11).

From Isaiah: " 'Cry loudly, do not hold back; raise your voice like a trumpet, and declare to My people their *transgression,* and to the house of Jacob (the church) their sins. Yet they seek Me day by day, and delight to know My ways, as a nation that has done righteousness (pretending obedience) and has not forsaken the ordinance (Word) of their God.' '... Why have we fasted and Thou dost not see?' … 'Behold, you fast for contention and strife …' " (Isa. 58:1-4).

" 'Is it a fast like this which I choose, a day for a man to humble himself? … Is this not the fast which I chose, *to loosen the bonds of wickedness,* to undo the bands of the yoke (set free from the bondage of the powers of darkness), and to let the oppressed go free, and break every yoke? Is it not to divide your bread (the Word of God) with the hungry, and bring the homeless poor into the house; when you see the naked (lost), to cover him (with garments of salvation); and not to hide yourself from your own flesh?' " (Isa. 58:5-7).

Isaiah continues: "Then your light (revelation, discernment, and enlightenment) will break out like the dawn, and your recovery will speedily spring forth (*restoration*); and your righteousness will go before you; the glory of the Lord will be your rear guard. Then you will call, and the Lord will answer; you will cry, and He will say, 'Here I am' (because your prayers will be answered). If you remove the yoke from your midst, the pointing of the finger (criticism, faultfinding, gossip, slander, etc.), and speaking wickedness (cursing your neighbor instead of loving him), and if you give yourself to the hungry (lay down your life), and satisfy the desire of the afflicted (by doing the works of Jesus), then your light will rise in darkness (veil removed from your eyes), and your gloom (darkness) will become like midday (full light)" (Isa. 58:8-10).

"And the Lord will continually guide you, and satisfy your desire (blessings) in scorched places (fiery trials), and give strength to your bones (healing); and you will be like a watered garden, and like a spring of water whose waters do not fail. And *those from among you will rebuild the ancient ruins* (build the wall and the temple); *you will raise up the age-old foundations* (the Word of God); and you will be called the *repairer of the breach, the restorer of the streets (the highways of holiness and righteousness)* in which to dwell" (Isa. 58:11, 12).

From Ezekiel: "Thus says the Lord God, 'When I gather the house of Israel (remnant) from the peoples among whom they are scattered, and shall manifest My holiness in them in the sight of the nations, then they will live in their land which I gave to My servant Jacob. And they will live in it securely; and they will build houses, plant vineyards, and live securely, when I execute judgments upon all who scorn them round about them. Then they will know that I am the Lord their God' " (Ezek. 28:25, 26).

From Zephaniah: "In that day you will feel no shame because of all your deeds by which you have rebelled against Me, for then I will remove from your midst (destroy) your proud, exulting ones, and you will never again be haughty on My holy mountain. But I will leave among you a humble and lowly people, and they will take refuge in the name of the Lord. The remnant of Israel will do no wrong and tell no lies, nor will a deceitful tongue be found in their mouths; for they shall feed and lie down (in peace) with no one to make them tremble (in fear because the remnant will have a hedge around them and they will walk in holiness and peace)" (Zeph. 3:11-13).

Again from Zephaniah: " 'In those days and at that time,' declares the Lord, 'the sons of Israel will come, both they and the sons of Judah as well; they will go along weeping as they go, and it will be the Lord their God they seek. They will ask for the way to Zion, turning their faces in its direction; they will come that they may join themselves to the Lord in an everlasting covenant that will not be forgotten. In those days and at that time,' declares the Lord, 'search will be made for the iniquity of Israel, but there will be none; and for the sins of Judah, but they will not be found; for I shall pardon those whom I leave as a remnant." (Jer. 50:4, 5, 20). "The Lord has taken away His judgments against you, He has cleared away your enemies. *THE KING OF ISRAEL,* the Lord, is in your midst; you will fear disaster no more" (Zeph. 3:15).

From Isaiah: "And it will come about that he who is left in Zion and remains in Jerusalem (the true church) will be called holy — everyone who is recorded for life in Jerusalem (the heavenly Jerusalem). When the Lord has washed away the filth of the daughters of Zion, and purged the bloodshed of Jerusalem (the heavenly Jerusalem) from her midst, by the *Spirit of judgment* and the *spirit of burning*" (Isa. 4:3, 4).

"Rouse yourself! ... Arise, O Jerusalem (church), you who have drunk from the Lord's hand the cup of His anger ..." (Isa. 51:17). "And I will put it into the hands of your *tormentors* (the powers of darkness), who have said to you, 'Lie down that we may walk over you.' You have even made your back like the ground, and like the street for those who walk over it" (Isa. 51:23).

"*AWAKE, AWAKE (SLEEPING VIRGINS),* Clothe yourself in your strength, O Zion (church) ... shake yourself from the dust, rise up, O captive Jerusalem (church) Loose yourself from the chains around your neck, O captive daughter of Zion (the church)" (Isa. 52:1, 2).

From Ezekiel: "... Surely because My flock has become a prey, My flock has even become food for all the beasts of the field (the powers of darkness) *for lack of a shepherd,* and My shepherds did not search for My flock, but rather the shepherds fed themselves and *did not feed My flock* ... Thus says the Lord God, 'Behold, *I am against the shepherds,* and I shall demand My sheep from them and make them cease from feeding sheep ... I shall deliver My flock from their mouth ..." (Ezek. 34:8, 10).

"For thus says the Lord God, 'Behold, I Myself will search for My sheep and seek them out ... and will deliver them from all the places to which they were scattered on a cloudy and gloomy day (of spiritual darkness). And I will bring them out from the peoples and gather them from the countries ... I will feed them in a good pasture ... there they will lie down (in peace and rest) in good grazing ground and they will feed in rich pasture on the mountains of Israel (Zion)' " (Ezek. 34:11-14).

From Jeremiah: "I shall also raise up shepherds over them and they will tend them; they will not be afraid any longer ..." (Jer. 23:4).

From Ezekiel: "I will make a covenant of peace with them and eliminate harmful beasts (powers of darkness) from the land ... I will make them and the places around My hill (presence of the Lord) a blessing. And I will cause showers of blessings. Also, the tree of the field will yield its fruit ... and they will be secure on their land. Then they will know that I am the Lord, when I have broken the bars of their yoke and delivered them from the hand of those who enslaved them. And they will no longer be a prey to the nations, and the beasts of the earth (powers of darkness) will not devour them; but they will live securely and no one will make them afraid" (Ezek. 23:25-28).

" 'I will feed My flock and I will lead them to rest,' declares the Lord God. 'I will seek the lost, bring back the scattered, bind up the broken, and strengthen the sick; but the fat and the strong I will destroy. I will feed them with judgment' " (Ezek. 34:15, 16).

From Jeremiah: "Set up for yourself roadmarks, place for yourself guideposts; direct your mind to the highway (of holiness) ... Return, O virgin of Israel, return to these your cities. Thus says the Lord of hosts, the God of Israel, 'Once again they will speak this word in the land of Judah and in its cities, when I restore their fortunes,' The Lord bless you, O abode of righteousness, O holy hill!" (Jer. 31:21, 23).

From Isaiah: "Listen! Your *WATCHMEN* (true shepherds) lift up their voices, they shout joyfully together; for they will see with their own eyes when the Lord restores Zion (the church)" (Isa. 52:8).

"Depart, depart, go out from there, touch nothing unclean; go out of the midst of her, *purify yourselves,* you who carry the vessels of the Lord" (Isa. 52:11).

"But Zion (the church) said, 'The Lord has forsaken me, and the Lord has forgotten me.' Can a woman forget her nursing child, and have no compassion on the son of her womb? Even these may forget, but I will never forget you. Behold, I have inscribed you on the palms of My hands (the nail prints of the cross). Your walls (My covenant promises to you) are continually before Me' " (Isa. 49:14-16).

The Psalmist wrote: "Then I said, 'Behold, I come; in the scroll of the book it is written of me; I delight to do Thy will, O my God; Thy law is within my heart' " (Ps. 40:7, 8).

From Isaiah: "A voice is calling, 'Clear the way for the Lord in the wilderness; make smooth in the desert a highway for our God. Let every valley be lifted up, and every mountain and hill be made low; and let the rough ground become a plain, and the rugged terrain a broad valley; then the glory of the Lord will be revealed, and all flesh will see it together; for the mouth of the Lord has spoken' " (Isa. 40:3-5).

From Revelation: "... Hallelujah! For the Lord Our God the Almighty reigns. Let us rejoice and be glad and give the glory to Him, for the marriage of the Lamb has come and *His bride has made herself ready* (pure, spotless, holy, and blameless). And it was given to her to clothe herself in fine linen, bright and clean; for the fine linen is the righteous acts of the saints" (Rev. 19:6-8).

" 'AND A REDEEMER WILL COME TO ZION, and TO THOSE (remnant) WHO TURN FROM TRANS- GRESSION IN JACOB (the church)' declares the Lord" (Isa. 59:20). "Get yourself up on a high mountain, O Zion, bearer of good news, lift up your voice mightily, O Jerusalem, bearer of good news; lift it up, do not fear. Say to the cities of Judah, 'Here is your God!' Behold, the Lord God will come with might, with His arm ruling for Him. Behold, His reward is with Him, and His recompense before Him. Like a shepherd He will tend His flock, in His arm He will gather the lambs, and carry them in His bosom; He will gently lead the nursing ewes" (Isa. 40:9-11).

Highway of Holiness

From Isaiah: "Encourage the exhausted, and strengthen the feeble. Say to those with anxious heart, 'Take courage, fear not. Behold, your God will come with vengeance; the recompense of God will come, but He will save you.' And a highway will be there, a roadway, and it will be called the *HIGHWAY OF HOLINESS*. The unclean (who walk after the flesh) will not travel on it, but it will be for him who walks that way (in holiness), and fools (with foolish hearts) will not wander on it. No lion (the powers of darkness) will be there, nor will any vicious beast go up on it; these will not be found there. But the redeemed will walk there, and *THE RANSOMED OF THE LORD WILL RETURN, AND COME WITH JOYFUL SHOUTING TO ZION, WITH EVERLASTING JOY UPON THEIR HEADS. THEY WILL FIND GLADNESS AND JOY, AND SORROW AND SIGHING WILL FLEE AWAY*" (Isa. 35:3, 4, 8-10).

"On your walls, O Jerusalem, I have appointed watch - men; all day and all night they will never keep silent. You who remind the Lord, take no rest for yourselves, and give Him no rest until He establishes and makes Jerusalem (the church) a praise in the earth. Go through, go through the gates; clear the way for the people; build up, build up the highway; remove the stones, *lift up a standard (the Word of God over the peoples)*. Behold, the Lord has proclaimed to the end of the earth, say to the daughter of Zion, 'Lo, your salvation comes; behold His reward is with Him, and His recompense before Him,' And they will call them *'The holy people, the redeemed of the Lord';* and you will be called, *'SOUGHT OUT, A CITY NOT FORSAKEN'* " (Isa. 62:6, 7, 10-12).

Daniel prayed: " 'So now, our God, listen to the prayer of Thy servant and to his supplications; and for Thy sake, O Lord, let Thy face shine on Thy desolate sanctuary. O my

God, incline Thine ear and hear! Open Thine eyes and see our desolations and the city which is called by Thy name; for we are not presenting our supplications before Thee on account of any merits of our own, but on account of Thy great compassion. O Lord, hear! O Lord, forgive! O Lord, listen and take action! For Thine own sake, O my God, do not delay, because Thy city and Thy people are called by Thy name' " (Dan. 9:17-19).

From Matthew: " 'O Jerusalem, Jerusalem, who ... stones those who are sent to her! ... Behold, your house is being left to you desolate! For I say to you, from now on *YOU SHALL NOT SEE ME UNTIL YOU SAY, 'BLESSED IS HE WHO COMES IN THE NAME OF THE LORD!'* " (Matt. 23:37-39).

Afterword

This book is humbly dedicated to the Lord Jesus Christ who came to me, when I was lost and dying, to give me life. Who gave me speech when I could no longer carry on a conversation. Who healed a body broken by drugs, alcohol, demons, and physical decay. Although I was a very unlovable man with no hope, He loved me and healed me.

To my Lord, Who did one of the most ridiculous things I have ever known. He took this same man, a carpet cleaner with a ninth grade education, and said, "I am choosing you as a vessel of grace; I am giving you a part." Who spoke to me in a deserted fishing camp in Florida and said, "Go and tell these people that they keep on listening but do not perceive, they keep on looking but do not understand."

I also humbly dedicate this book to His Godly shepherds and Godly craftsmen who are presently forsaking all to become the instruments to build the temple of God in unity and purpose, holy and blameless, giving glory to no one but our Lord.

I lay this book at Your feet, Lord. I pray for much more of your abundant mercy, grace, and wisdom, lest after I have now shared with others, I become a castaway. Also, please bless the ones who have walked with me and helped me, especially my loving wife, Joyce, and my brother in Christ, Rick, and those who pray for me. I love you, Lord, beyond any words and I now trust You to bless as You change the heart and life of each person who reads this book.

Publisher's Note:
The publishers recognize the great spiritual depth of this book. Therefore, in order that you might fully grasp the message herein, we seriously suggest that you read the book again.

—The Publishers

Milton Green
Audio & Video Tapes

Audio tapes are a wonderful way to share God's Word and truth. It is our desire to minister to your spiritual needs, not to sell or peddle the Word of our Lord. We simply want to make you aware of the materials available just as we do for those who attend "In the Word" meetings.

Many people are unaware of the expense involved in production and ask what they should contribute for the tapes. The amount suggested is usually $2 per tape. Some contribute more, and some give less because they cannot afford as much. The ones who contribute more help cover our production costs and enable us to freely share the Word with those who are unable to afford the tapes.

If you have financial problems and cannot afford to help cover the cost of the tapes, please let us know. It is our desire to help build you up and help you become a success in our Lord Jesus Christ. Let the Spirit of the Lord guide you as we all build treasures in heaven.

The Eternal Gospel: Revealed in These Last Days
 (recorded December 1986)   (20 tapes)
How We Prepare to Come Out and Meet the Bridegroom
 (recorded April 1987)   (16 tapes)
Saved Through the Fire (recorded August 1987) (15 tapes)
Joshua and Caleb Meeting (recorded December 1987) (12 tapes)
How the Church Has Failed to Fulfill God's Law (10 tapes)
What is True Salvation?   (10 tapes)

How We Make Covenant (Formerly titled,
    "The Church Today ... Asleep and in Bondage")   (10 tapes)
The Broad Road to Destruction   (2 tapes)
Babylon: The Church in the Last Days   (14 tapes)
The Law and Holiness, Volume I   (12 tapes)
The Law and Holiness, Volume II   (12 tapes)
The Mark of God or the Mark of the Beast   (2 tapes)
How God's Kind of Love is Perfected in You   (12 tapes)
How We Lay Down Our Lives to Love Others   (2 tapes)
The Original "In the Word" Seminar   (16 tapes)
    (This series also available on video cassette)
Our Covenant with the Lord Jesus Christ   (5 tapes)
Healing in the Old and New Covenant   (3 tapes)
The Walk of Peace   (2 tapes)
Shrinking Back to Destruction and Fiery Trials   (4 tapes)
Close to Being Cursed   (3 tapes)
Illegitimate Sons   (4 tapes)
The God Kind of Love   (4 tapes)
Personal Testimony   (1 tape)
The Pure Heart   (16 tapes)

VIDEO SERIES

The original "In the Word" Seminar is available on video cassette (twelve cassettes containing a total of 20½ hours of teaching). You may order the complete series of twelve tapes in two six-place albums with a donation of $195 or the tapes are available individually with a donation of $15 per tape. Other video series include:

available with donation of:

Sanctification: How Christ Is Formed in You *(three video cassettes containing six one-hour messages,* $42.75

The Schemes of Satan *(three video cassettes containing six one-hour messages)* $42.75

The Great Deception by Satan Today *(three video cassettes containing six one-hour messages)* $42.75